Virginia Cary Hudson
The *Jigs & Juleps!* Girl:
Her Life and Writings

Also by Beverly Kienzle

The Solutions to 38 Questions of Hildegard of Bingen (translator)

A Handbook to Hildegard of Bingen (coeditor)

A Handbook to Catherine of Siena (coeditor)

The Gospel Homilies of Hildegard of Bingen (translator)

Hildegard of Bingen and Her Gospel Homilies: Speaking New Mysteries

Expositiones evangeliorum by Hildegard of Bingen (coeditor)

Cistercians, Heresy and Crusade (1145–1229): Preaching in the Lord's Vineyard

The Sermon (editor)

Women Preachers and Prophets Through Two Millennia of Christianity (coeditor)

Medieval Sermons and Society: Cloister, City, University (coeditor)

Models of Holiness in Medieval Sermons (coeditor)

Sermons for the Summer Season: Liturgical Sermons from Rogationtide and Pentecost by Bernard of Clairvaux (translator)

De Ore Domini: Preacher and Word in the Middle Ages (coeditor)

Virginia Cary Hudson

The *Jigs & Juleps!* Girl:
Her Life and Writings

Beverly Mayne Kienzle

VIRGINIA CARY HUDSON
THE JIGS & JULEPS! GIRL: HER LIFE AND WRITINGS

iUniverse books may be ordered through booksellers or by contacting:

iUniverse
1663 Liberty Drive
Bloomington, IN 47403
www.iuniverse.com
1-800-Authors (1-800-288-4677)

ISBN: 978-1-4917-8781-6 (sc)
ISBN: 978-1-4917-8782-3 (hc)
ISBN: 978-1-4917-8780-9 (e)

Library of Congress Control Number: 2016904817

Print information available on the last page.

iUniverse rev. date: 6/3/2016

For my beloved mother, Virginia Cleveland Mayne—
May the angels place this book beside her on a heavenly cloud.

Contents

Preface

As I brought this book to a conclusion after more than twenty-five years of work, I gained a sense of peace and of blessing. I had relived more than a century of my grandmother's and my mother's joys and sorrows. Fatigue pushed against my will, but I had promised to complete what my mother began—to prove that Virginia Cary Hudson had lived and that her adult writings exhibited the spirit and the faith that she had displayed at the age of ten. Once I neared the end, I realized how greatly the blessings overshadowed the losses. I recalled my grandmother's words that "God holds in His hand, / a dipper of stars, / filled with blessings, / intended for you." Indeed, to complete this book, to fulfill my mother's intention, and to receive the blessings poured out on my life would not have been possible without the support bestowed by close family and friends who accompanied me on the journey.

My grandmother, my mother, and my auntie Ann kept nearly everything. My father ensured that I received the whole of my mother's belongings, and Auntie left me in charge of all her possessions. I inherited papers and photographs that alone would fill a nine-by-twelve-foot room. In this book I utilize writings from both my grandmother and mother, with a few references to Auntie's diary. My grandmother's writings appear completely unedited, and I have corrected only obvious spelling and punctuation errors in my mother's writing for clarity. Digital resources have multiplied enormously during the last decade, even during the last five years, when health problems limited my travel. Each time I searched for archives, I found something that was newly available and added it to my sources. I needed to stop writing, however, or I would continue updating and never actually publish the book. Moreover, no supporting document I could find would match the richness of the family materials I inherited.

I came to be grateful for the many papers and photos, and I am especially grateful to my family members for preserving our family history. That preservation would not have been possible without my father, Lewis, and my husband, Edward. These two strong and steadfast men embraced those material treasures, boxing, sorting, moving, and keeping them safe from Kentucky to Maryland to Florida to Connecticut to New York and to several places in Massachusetts. In the early 1990s, my father added his notes to my first drafts on events of the 1960s. My cherished husband has restored my energy for writing many times, accompanying me in reading the original sources and commenting on countless drafts of the book's chapters. Kathleen, our daughter, has joined the reading and proofreading. We delight in the character traits and turns of expression she shares with her great-grandmother. Our animal companions—Mia, the small dog; the kitty cats Athena, Cecilia, Stella, and Ruby; and the now-departed felines Basile, Tecla, and Walter—would gather around to welcome my rest breaks.

Friends and family have encouraged and supported my writing in various ways, from engaging in interested conversations to compiling sources to sorting and retouching photos to reading sections of the manuscript. I am grateful to Christopher Jarvinen, Darlene Slagle, Anita Dana, Linn Maxwell Keller, Jenny Bledsoe, Katherine Wrisley Shelby, Margaret Kienzle (my sister-in-law), Alison More, Robert Hensley King, Margaret Studier, Becky Scott, George Ferzoco, Carolyn A. Muessig, Jenny Brinsdon, John and Jane Gould, Peter Howard, Judith Rhodes and Martha Hughes, Priscilla Dewey Houghton, Jan and Eugene Ward, Ylva Hagman, Daniela Müller, Anne Brenon-Gasc, Robert Franklin, and Gustavo Pérez Firmat. I am also grateful to Hunt's Photos in Cambridge, Massachusetts, for restoring the photo of my grandmother in her twenties. I appreciate greatly the meticulous, thoughtful, and challenging feedback on my manuscript that the editors at iUniverse provided. My principal editor, although anonymous, initiated a constructive dialogue that influenced the flow and tone of my writing. Kathi Wittkamper, Editorial Consultant, and Steve Osikowicz, Publishing Services

Associate, deserve special gratitude and praise for their careful and highly responsive direction during the editorial and production process.

Finally, tracing my grandmother's trips from Louisville to Johns Hopkins in Baltimore sharpened my awareness of chronic pain as a factor in her life's journey and mine. It reinforced my sense of blessing that I live a short distance from the research hospitals in Boston. I am grateful to my physicians, especially Simon Weitzman, Paul Dellaripa, Zacharia Isaac, and Samardeep Gupta; to all the staff at the Brigham and Women's Hospital infusion center in Boston; and to my physical therapists at the Brigham and Women's Hospital and the Spaulding Rehabilitation Hospital. Through their help, along with my husband's and my daughter's faithful and indefatigable support, I have moved from the painful shock of rheumatoid arthritis to manageable life and work in the spirit of my grandmother's poem "Enjoy All the Good Things Now."

Virginia Cary Hudson Cleveland, twenty-two years old, with
Virginia Cleveland, six months old, on her lap, spring 1917

Introduction

Say your prayers and keep trying.

—Virginia Hudson Cleveland

A fifty-page book of a child's essays, selling for $2.50, made the first of sixty-six appearances on the *New York Times* Best Sellers list on May 27, 1962. The author, Virginia Cary Hudson, was my grandmother, who wrote the charming compositions as a ten-year-old in her Kentucky school. Her mother, Jessie Gregory Hudson, kept the original essays in a chintz-covered scrapbook that perished in a 1952 attic fire. My mother, Virginia Cleveland Mayne, had preserved copies of the originals five months before the fire. After my grandmother's death, my mother tried unsuccessfully for several years to find a publisher. Eventually a bishop's wife contacted literary agents she knew in Washington, DC, and the Macmillan Company agreed to publish the essays for my mother as *O Ye Jigs & Juleps!* After the success of *O Ye Jigs & Juleps!,* my mother prepared and published three more collections of my grandmother's writings: her adult essays, *Credos and Quips* (Macmillan Company, 1964) and *Close Your Eyes When Praying* (Harper & Row, 1968), and a selection of letters, *Flapdoodle, Trust & Obey* (Harper & Row, 1966). A swirling decade of manuscripts, book talks, and travels engaged my mother. The rapid publication of the books meant that my mother's talks on the three subsequent books often overlapped with the public appearances regarding *O*

Ye Jigs & Juleps! Her dream of making known my grandmother's extraordinary gifts came true at a whirlwind pace.

The love between mother and daughter radiates from the photograph shown on page xii. In the spring of 1917, my grandmother, twenty-two years old, holds my mother, six months old, on her lap. My grandmother painted the birds on the small canvas on the upper left wall in the photo. The precious painting, now in my apartment, connects me and my daughter to those loving women who came before us.

Virginia Cary Hudson's love of writing was nurtured by a sensitive teacher. A precocious child, Virginia stuttered, but her teacher noticed her talent with the written word and encouraged her to write her assignments instead of delivering them orally. Writing became a lifelong passion for Virginia. It gave her the means to capture the moments she experienced and share them. It also allowed her to preach and teach at religious groups and women's gatherings. She continued to fear stuttering and to guard against it by writing. My mother put it this way:

> The adult Virginia Cary Hudson Cleveland continued to write down whatever she planned to say and not just that, but her many reflections on life. One of her adult letters reads: "Tomorrow night at the Business Women's Church dinner I am to be the speaker. Hell, if I tried to speak, I would stammer so I would collapse. *Will have to read what I have to say.*"

This "safety valve of writing," as my mother described it, "was a life-long practice." It enabled my grandmother, as she put it, to "read what I have to say," and it made possible our reading of what she did have to say. Her many thoughts on Christian history and the Bible were expressed in talks at church, and some were published in *Credos & Quips*. As detailed in my mother's notes, Virginia "was always writing something for her programs of Christian Education. Often she read to my husband and me whatever her latest happened to be. Many of her notes [appeared] on the back of checks; any pieces of paper, mother wrote on [them]." When she completed stories of her experiences, she would mail them to my mother or deliver them in person when she visited or when we came to Kentucky. In a letter to my mother, she said, "I have your story, bring the first series back with you, and I will put them together in a scrapbook, for you to keep." She mentioned that she was "doing some pages on the Cary's," her father's Virginia ancestors. She also said, "By the way I am writing a story of the Bible and dedicating it to Beverly. It is for children." My mother begged my grandmother to have the essays from the attic published. "She was always going to call somebody, who knew somebody, who was going to call ... Oh! heavens you know what happened with such plans as this—Nothing," wrote my mother.

Virginia published nothing during her lifetime, but she wrote constantly. In a time before inexpensive telephone lines and long before e-mail, letters allowed the fullest communication possible with her grown daughter, who had moved from Louisville to Washington, DC. These letters conveyed frequent updates from home, episodes from family history, and my grandmother's aspiration to publish. She wrote in one letter that someday she was "going to write a book and call it 'The Chest'" and in it "put all the rollicking pathos and humor" of all the southern lore and doings that she knew. She vowed, "If I can, I am going to make the hair of every Yankee who reads it stand on end, and who knows, it might be published."

Virginia Cary Hudson Cleveland's adult writings included some hair-raising tales, many religious essays, letters, notes for talks, poems, essays, fables, drawings, my scrapbook with the title "Sitting and Thinking," and even more. The second and fourth published books of her work, *Credos & Quips* and *Close Your Eyes When Praying*, present selections from this large collection of writings—typed and handwritten—that were arranged in composition books as well as jotted down on the backs of envelopes. As my mother explained in "Ah, Dear Readers," the narrative of her own that she began but did not finish for publication,

Mother was determined that someday she would write a book. She talked of this continuously, but for her that someday never came. Yet she did a great deal of writing, using whatever scraps of paper might be available when inspired moments came or when she agreed to give a talk at a church or mission.

Out of more than two hundred letters that my mother saved, eighteen were published in *Flapdoodle, Trust & Obey.* My grandmother confided in my mother her aspirations to do more writing and to publish. Many things got in the way, but she kept writing about whatever happened to her, even the fire.

In October 1952, the third floor and attic burst into flames at 1453 St. James Court, Louisville, Kentucky. I have no memories of the fire occurring. My mother wrote an account of what she learned from letters and calls between Kentucky and Maryland.

Early in October, I believe to be exact it was the eighth day of the month, the year 1952 and very early in the morning, my sister smelled smoke. She went down to the second floor and called my mother. It was then that the Louisville fire department was called. They arrived, went over the house, but couldn't find anything alarming. While they were standing in the second floor hallway talking to mother, the attic section under the roof burst into flames. One of her letters describes this, and it reads "the whole roof burst into a mass of flames with a roar that sounded like an explosion."

When the fire chief arrived, my grandmother sat silently. When he asked if she would feel better if she spoke, she replied, "I told him I was talking all the time, talking to the Lord."[1] My mother attempted to describe the impacts of the fire:

You can well imagine what happened to the old trunks, grandmother's beautifully and carefully wrapped contents, the chintz-covered scrapbook and the rest. They were gone, and very quickly. The water damage to the entire house was horrible. Without a shadow of a doubt this event shortened my mother's life, but even in the face of all this destruction the closing sentence of her letter read, "By Christmas everything should be in order."

My mother then wrote to ask if my grandmother's writings had been destroyed. My grandmother replied on the back of the pages of the letter she had received,

> The things I have written—some here—some yonder—some God knows where. Will get them together for you. If you care to rise and shine in the Auxiliary, you may use my "talks." You may get mobbed. If they kill you, you won't have to pay your bills. Lewis can dress up on your insurance.

The October letter about the fire goes on to say that my grandfather and Joe Rogers, his old friend and business partner, had left the morning of the sixteenth for Waterford Park in Wheeling, where they were to race Devil's Grin. Another horse, Lacuna, was expected to win the next time out at five-eighths of a mile. But two more terrible events occurred: another fire that killed several horses and an accident that injured my grandfather. As my mother recounted,

> Ten days after this fire, my father's horses stabled at Waterford Park in West Virginia burned. Returning to Kentucky in his automobile, he had an accident and broke his chest bone.

My grandmother provided more detail in her letter:

> Your father and Joe reached Waterford just in time to find it in flames and about eight hundred horses running wild, turned out of the flaming stables. All of Joe's horses burned up, including Devil's Grin and the two-year old I saw in Canada who was the most

beautiful horse I ever saw. His name was Perfect Idea, and I have never seen anything in a Derby parade that would hold a candle to him. Driving home, with nothing left, they had a bad wreck out of Steubensville, Ohio, tore the car up, were taken to the hospital.

Virginia had written earlier in the fall about Devil's Grin and his ability to make wide turns without losing speed. She'd also spoken of a horseman in Canada who coveted the handsome and swift Perfect Idea and who had pressured "Mr. Joe" to sell him. Mr. Joe had refused, and Perfect Idea perished in the tragic fire.[2] A story in the October 17, 1952, *Pittsburgh Post-Gazette* reported that 792 horses fled in all directions, one stable hand perished, and five horses were burned while five others were injured.[3] Exactly how many of these horses belonged to my grandfather or to Mr. Joe I do not know, but from my grandmother's words, the fire must have raged quickly in their area of the stable. Was it an act of God or a case of arson?

When my mother and I arrived on the train for our Christmas visit in December 1952, my grandmother managed to greet us with a humorous anecdote about the fire. My mother summarized it as follows:

> It seems that my father had hired two men to slap paint onto the back of the house. The kitchen section of the Saint James Court house extended out from the main body of the house … The fire department worked with large hoses up the front center hall steps and on to the steps leading to the third floor to keep the flames from spreading to the second floor. In the meantime any and every thing that could be thrown out the windows was thrown. Furniture was carried out and set down. Water to quell the flames ran every place; the axing that was necessary was performed. Bedding sailed out the windows landing on bushes or on the ground. Clothes followed and as more firemen

arrived, they carried out all carryable objects, should the flames not be quelled. Virginia glanced out into the back yard and against the extended section of the house were two ladders with two painters happily at work, painting away regardless. Articles were sailing over their heads, firemen were running everywhere, fire hoses were extended, but those souls had sworn to show up to paint and this is just what they were doing.

Swearing to Kirtley S. Cleveland, known as Mr. K. S., that a job would be done meant serious business, enough to keep the painters working out of fear in the midst of fire and flying furniture.

Less than two years later, Virginia's life ended suddenly just before her sixtieth birthday. My mother vowed to publish my grandmother's childhood essays and other captivating writings, including the scrapbook of poems and drawings my grandmother had made for me after the fire. Publishing my grandmother's works would achieve a victory against destruction and loss. After many rejection letters and innumerable prayers, four books were published by major presses.

In the frequent talks my mother gave at book signings for O Ye Jigs & Juleps! and for the other books, she was compelled to answer questions that shocked, angered, and hurt her so deeply: Had Virginia Cary Hudson really existed? Had she really written the essays in O Ye Jigs & Juleps!? Could my mother prove there had been a damaging fire? My mother obtained a letter (July 26, 1962) from Citizens Fidelity Insurance Company to certify that the fire occurred. The letter's author recalled that he himself "came out with an adjuster and arranged for settlement and repairs."[4] Aware and wary of the damage that could be done to treasured papers, my mother entrusted the pages from my grandmother's letters about the fire to the Kentucky Historical Society.[5]

Most readers of my grandmother's writings want to know more about Virginia Cary Hudson's life—her childhood; her family;

her marriage to a thoroughbred horse trainer; her teaching and preaching in Louisville, Kentucky; and her travels to racetracks in the United States, Cuba, Mexico, and Canada. Her warmth and humor delighted family and friends all her life. She empathized with the joys and sorrows of the people around her. She grasped the essence of their individuality and expressed it not only in the essays she wrote as a child but also in her adult talks for church audiences and in the many letters she wrote. Sharing memories of my grandmother's life will, I hope, delight readers and quiet doubters who contested—much to my mother's heartbreak—whether Virginia Cary Hudson ever lived or wrote the childhood essays in *O Ye Jigs & Juleps!*, the very writings that my mother discovered in my great-grandmother's trunk in the attic at St. James Court in 1952.

My mother was determined to answer the skeptics with a biography of Virginia Cary Hudson, with the story of publishing her writings, and with the publication of my scrapbook and the letters to me. However, Alzheimer's disease sadly brought her work to a halt. This volume carries forward the work that my mother began. It represents the first biography of Virginia Cary Hudson and contains works of hers published for the very first time: prayers, letters to me from 1951 to 1954, and the scrapbook she made for me and brought to Maryland in the summer of 1953.

Timeline for Virginia Cary Hudson Cleveland's Life and Writings

May 28, 1894—Virginia Cary Hudson is born in Versailles, Kentucky, the only child of Jessie G. Hudson and Richard N. Hudson V.

She spends her childhood in Cloverport and then Versailles with secondary residence in Louisville.

She attends Margaret Hall School, Versailles, and the Bristol School for Girls, Washington, DC.

May 7, 1914—Virginia marries Kirtley S. Cleveland at St. John's Episcopal Church, Versailles.

January 1915—R. N. Hudson is elected president of the L. H. & St. L. Railway.

1915–1923—R. N. Hudson has country home built near Cloverport, with private airplane landing.

November 21, 1916—Virginia Hudson Cleveland, Virginia's first daughter, is born.

January 25, 1920—Ann Cary Cleveland, Virginia's second daughter, is born.

1922—Virginia Cary Hudson Cleveland spends the summer in Cloverport and teaches Sunday school.

1923—Photos are taken of Virginia's two daughters in Cloverport during the summer.

Virginia divorces and remarries Kirtley S. Cleveland.

January 1928—Virginia and family spend the winter in Cuba.

1929—L. H. & St. L. is consolidated with L & N. R. N. Hudson becomes staff officer for operation of the L & N.

January 17, 1930—Richard Hudson Cleveland, Virginia's first son and third child, is born. K. S. Cleveland is in Cuba.

1930—Per the census, Virginia and family reside at 30 Reeser Street, Louisville.

October 1936—Virginia and family take up residence at 1439 St. James Court, Louisville.

December 19, 1936—R. N. Hudson has his last meal at Pendennis Club.

January 1937—The great flood strikes Louisville.

January 25, 1937—R. N. Hudson dies.

February 10, 1937—R. N. Hudson is buried in Cloverport.

July 8, 1938—Jessie G. Hudson purchases 1453 St. James Court, Louisville.

1939 to 1954—Virginia serves as secretary and treasurer and then president of the St. James Court Association.

January 22, 1942—Jessie G. Hudson dies.

1948–1954—Virginia gives talks to Women's Auxiliary at Calvary Episcopal Church and to adult Sunday classes.

Thursday, April 8, 1954—Virginia dies.

Easter Monday, April 12, 1954—Virginia's funeral is held at Olsen Funeral Home.

Easter Monday, April 16, 1962—*O Ye Jigs & Juleps!* is published.

May 27, 1962—*O Ye Jigs & Juleps!* appears on the *New York Times* Best Sellers list.

June 8, 1964—Virginia (daughter) gives presentation of *Credos &
Quips* at American Booksellers' Association convention.

February 17, 1966—*Flapdoodle, Trust & Obey* is published.

1968—*Close Your Eyes When Praying* is published.

Chapter One

Virginia Cary Hudson and Her Family

ho was Virginia Cary Hudson? The "best newspaper woman in New York"? A "widow who earned a precarious living"?[6] The fabrication of a skillful editor or a clever daughter? Reviewers and publicity stretched my grandmother's identity. She never visited New York City, nor was she ever a widow. She certainly lived, and she undoubtedly authored the works ascribed to her. In this chapter I will recount what I know of her life and will answer the challenges to her genuineness that linger despite the publication of her four books and even among some admirers of *O Ye Jigs & Juleps!*

My mother stated simply and repeatedly in her notes for "Ah, Dear Readers," "There was a ten-year-old Southern girl whose father was with a railroad, and who attended a Church boarding school" and "The girl whose name was Virginia Cary Hudson grew up and when she was twenty, she married Kirtley S. Cleveland and bore him two daughters and a son." Those were perhaps the opening lines of the many talks my mother gave about *O Ye Jigs & Juleps!*, *Credos & Quips*, *Close Your Eyes When Praying*, and *Flapdoodle, Trust & Obey*. Bookstores around the country issued speaking invitations to her, as did Episcopal church groups and women's clubs. The Macmillan Company and Harper & Row arranged travel and promotional tours for her. At each place my mother gave a presentation about the book(s), followed by a question-and-answer session. My mother tucked her typed and handwritten notes into copies of the four books, along with special bookmarks and small envelopes filled with the many four-leaf clovers she found and saved for as long as I can remember. Some index cards inside the books were typed, numbered, and keyed to tabbed pages. My mother undoubtedly used those references to be ready for questions. I find them handy myself. Taken together, the notes, the books, and the many folders of letters, photos, and clippings provide rich resources for a biography of Virginia and a history of her writings. The material falls into three categories: Virginia's youth and family, her marriage and travels with her husband, and her last decade of life.

A Child with Sparkling Eyes and a Stutter: Virginia's Childhood

Virginia Cary Hudson at three months old, August 1894

The sparkle in Virginia's eyes in photos, even as a three-month-old child, seems to foreshadow the promise of her talents. The only child of Jessie Lee Gregory Hudson and Richard Nathaniel Hudson V, Virginia was born in Louisville, Kentucky, on May 28, 1894, several years after her parents' marriage on December 26, 1889. Jessie began her life in Cloverport, Kentucky, on September 1, 1867. At the time of the 1880 census, Jessie's father, John D. Gregory, was forty years old and was the wharfmaster; Jessie's mother, Eliza, was thirty-two; and Jessie was twelve, the oldest of four siblings.[7] An old photo given to me by my auntie Ann shows a large home in Cloverport, with a note on the back written in my great-grandmother's hand: "Our House in Cloverport."[8] Perhaps this was the Gregory home.

Jessie Lee Gregory, ca. 1887

Family house, probably in Cloverport, Kentucky, undated

The formal portrait below of Virginia at seventeen months old was taken in Louisville around November 1895. Her partial smile and her playful gaze seem to say that she enjoys the frills and the artificial pose but not for long. The photograph below of Virginia outdoors at age three shows a strong-minded child. She smiles somewhat reluctantly, with a twinkle in her eye as she places her arms and hands over her stiff petticoat. In another scene, Virginia

Virginia Cary Hudson at seventeen months old, in Louisville, Kentucky, November 1895

Virginia Cary Hudson, age three, 1897

and her mother, Jessie, ride with their driver in a horse-drawn carriage with two dogs close at hand (p. 4). Given Virginia's age, around two or perhaps three years old, one of the dogs may be

Daniel, whose obituary appeared in the *Breckenridge News* on June 6, 1900.[9] Virginia's family moved from Cloverport to Versailles during her childhood, but they visited her grandmother (Jessie's mother, Eliza Gregory) in Cloverport (*O Ye Jigs and Juleps!*, 34–35). The Hudsons later kept an additional residence in Louisville.

*Jessie Gregory Hudson and Virginia Cary Hudson riding
in a horse-drawn carriage, ca. 1896–1897*

Jessie was said to have kept her hat on all day so that she would always be ready to accept an invitation to go out, wherever she was. A Louisville reviewer and family friend wrote that Mrs. Cleveland (Virginia Cary Hudson) "usually dressed in striking fashion" and conjectured that this trait was perhaps inherited from Jessie. "Grandmother Hudson loved parties and was always ready to go to them," the reviewer wrote, and to speed her departure she usually wore a hat around the house. According to the family friend, hats figured in the memories of another Louisvillian, who had made many visits to the Cleveland home and who recalled, "I never saw Mrs. Hudson without her hat—even when she was dusting."[10] The elaborate hat Jessie wears in the carriage photo, or one similar to it, appears in another photo from around the same time.

The best-known image of Virginia is the portrait taken when she was ten years old (p. 6), the age when she wrote the essays that became *O Ye Jigs & Juleps!* Her aunt preserved the photo in a trunk, and the aunt's daughter discovered it just after the book's publication.

My mother wrote the following about my grandmother's school days in Versailles:

Jessie Gregory Hudson wearing a hat, ca. 1896

> She was bright and high-spirited, but she stuttered and found it difficult to speak in school, and a teacher who tried hard to help this child, allowed her to write out her assignments. She wrote them so well that nobody could have imagined that she had trouble expressing herself. Her mother, my grandmother, saved the little pieces and put them in a chintz-covered scrapbook.

Jessie must have treasured the essays Virginia wrote all the more since she knew her daughter's struggles at formal oral expression. When Virginia spoke publicly as an adult, she still wrote out the text of what she planned to say. She grew to love writing, channeling her keen observations, deep feelings, and clever humor into written form.

Where did Virginia meet the kind teacher who discerned her gifts and influenced her life? The teacher doubtless worked at Margaret Hall School for Girls (once called Margaret College), founded in

Virginia Cary Hudson, ten years old, 1904

1891 in Versailles, Kentucky, and later run by the Episcopal Sisters of St. Helena. Instruction probably involved frequent recitation and numerous oral reports. English classes may have been divided into writing and oral English, a child's entry into public speaking. It seems likely that Virginia's teacher allowed her to substitute some written work for oral presentations. Virginia attended Margaret Hall and, later, another Episcopal school in Washington, DC, the Bristol School for Girls. My mother noted that my grandmother was at the Bristol School in 1912, for my grandmother recalled that she, with other girls and a teacher, toured the White House that winter.[11]

I have no records from Virginia's school days. They were probably stored in Jessie's trunk and destroyed in the 1952 fire. I do have a French text that she used, Prosper Mérimée's novella *Colomba*, suitable for an advanced course in secondary school. What I found remarkable in this copy are the drawings. Virginia loved to draw. Her letters are filled with simple drawings, and I have a few of her ink drawings, watercolors, and oil paintings. This product from young womanhood reveals an exquisite imagination in pen-and-ink drawings. Each of the characters has a portrait, and Virginia captured some scenes from the novella. The young Colomba, with thick chestnut hair swept upward, bears a distinct resemblance to the artist. The novella's theme of Colomba's pride in her father and will to avenge his death must have appealed to a daughter who loved her father so deeply.

Virginia recalled the Bristol School in an essay published in *Credos & Quips*:

> Once, a long time ago, I was sent away to a very expensive school. I expected something exciting and very fancy. I thought that I was going to have myself one big time, but I found things very different from what I expected. I found in that school things of everlasting worth; the combination of simple truth and unbiased thinking. Above the classroom door was a motto in large gold letters. After all these years,

> I can still see it. It read, "Politeness is to do and say the kindest thing in the kindest way." (*Credos*, 34)

Why did Virginia depart for Washington, DC, to finish her education? Perhaps her parents sought a year of finishing school for her so that she would meet people of influence? At that point, her father's career was rising in the railroad. Perhaps they wanted to send Virginia not only to Washington but away from Versailles. At age sixteen, so sometime between May 1910 and May 1911, Virginia eloped with someone. I know only that he had red hair and was not Kirtley S. Cleveland, the man she married in 1914. Kirtley, about eight years older than Virginia, had watched her from the time she was in pigtails and had decided that he wanted her for his own bride. The night of the elopement, he saw Virginia and the would-be bridegroom fleeing in a carriage and called the constable. She was arrested and brought home.

A Railroad President's Daughter

Virginia's love for her father radiates from the essays of *O Ye Jigs & Juleps!* She regularly waited for him on the railroad platform until he arrived home. His demeanor was reserved, in contrast to her mother's emotive reactions, and his English accent so pronounced that her friends could barely understand him (*Jigs*, 35, 37). Richard was born in Virginia during the Civil War (March 29, 1864) to Ann (or Anne) Cary and Richard N. Hudson IV. A two-sided glass frame in my home preserves an 1850 letter from Ann's mother, Harriet Cary, granting permission for Ann and Richard's marriage. I also have the wedding ring, engraved with the initials and the date, June 4, 1850. Richard N. Hudson IV (1810–1890), born in Manchester, England,[12] arrived in New York in 1831 and then settled in Virginia as a farmer/dentist (1860 census). After the Civil War, he practiced dentistry in the Monroe District of Richmond (1870 census). His son, Richard V, my great-grandfather, attended the English and Classical School in Richmond. By 1880, Ann Cary had died, and her husband had moved out of Richmond and into Louisa County.[13] My great-grandfather studied engineering and attended Eastman College in Poughkeepsie, New York. An autograph book contains the signatures of his classmates at Eastman—a fine historical display of penmanship.[14]

My grandmother and my mother served actively in the Daughters of the American Revolution, taking great pride in their ancestors, some of whom aided the American War of Independence, while others remained loyalists. My mother attended the DAR national conventions as a page and then as a delegate for Kentucky, guarding the pins and ribbons she wore for those occasions among her treasured keepsakes. Only in writing this book have I come to understand that the family pride in the DAR, which I did not join as an adult, took its roots in the love and honor inspired by my great-grandfather and his family members.

Virginia's grandmother Ann Cary (1825–1879) was a descendant of the influential Cary family of Virginia. Ann's ancestry traces to "the immigrant" Miles Cary (ca. 1622–1667), who sailed from Bristol, England, to Virginia, first appearing in the Warwick County, Virginia, records in 1645.[15] From Ann, Cary furniture passed to my great-grandfather, my grandmother, my mother, my aunt, and me. Hudson furniture accompanied it. My grandmother and mother wrote descriptions and eventually had photos taken of the historic pieces, silent but powerful reminders of our heritage.

Richard N. Hudson V, born
March 29, 1864

Richard Cary, our key DAR ancestor, served as a member of important bodies in Virginia history, including the 1776 convention that framed the Virginia Declaration of Rights.[16] Letters and legends tie another Cary to George Washington. Sarah Cary, known as Sally, the granddaughter of Miles Cary (1655–1708) and Mary Wilson, married George William Fairfax, but she is remembered as the woman George Washington loved before he married Martha Custis.[17]

My grandmother composed a history of the Carys for her children. On its handwritten pages she weaves together genealogy and intriguing stories such as Sally's. My grandmother relied on sources now lost: writings by Harriet Staples Cary, her paternal great-grandmother; letters from Sally Cary Fairfax that Harriet possessed but that Jessie Hudson burned once they were in her possession; and a portrait of Sally that Jessie chopped up with an axe! As a teenager, I reacted to these tales with disbelief. Now I realize the historical worth of what Jessie destroyed, and I wish I knew more about her character. She purportedly wanted to obliterate any possible influence that Sally and her lasting affection for George Washington, another woman's husband, could have on her granddaughters.[18] Jessie's harshness emerges in this story as in some essays included in *O Ye Jigs and Juleps!* about when she imposed harsh discipline on her daughter.

In 1887, R. N. Hudson moved to Kentucky and began to work with the Louisville, Henderson, and St. Louis Railway Company (then known as the Louisville, St. Louis and Texas Railway Company) as resident engineer in Cloverport. R. N. Hudson had worked on various engineering sites in Virginia, and he helped construct the 1927 Tombigbee River Bridge in Jackson, Alabama, for which he was the resident engineer.[19] As proudly noted in Jessie Hudson's handwritten obituary for her husband, "In early manhood he came to Kentucky with Col. Patton of [the] celebrated Civil Engineers."[20] William MacFarland Patton (1845–1905), an ancestor of General George S. Patton Jr., studied at what is now Virginia Tech, where he later became a professor. According to Patton's biography, "he spent … five years as the top engineer in bridge construction projects for various railway companies." Under his direction bridges were built across numerous rivers, including the Susquehanna, Ohio, Schuylkill, Warrior, Tombigbee, and Mobile Rivers. He also engineered the building of a railway between New Orleans and Mobile, Alabama, which was considered "one of the most difficult and complete engineering schemes in the country."[21] R. N. Hudson worked west and south from Virginia to Kentucky and beyond with Patton's engineers. My great-grandfather became roadmaster and chief resident engineer before being named general manager of the Louisville and Atlantic Railroad on January 1, 1906.

Virginia and her children would have traversed bridges that R. N. Hudson helped build. Jessie kept pictures or remembrances of his accomplishments for all to see. "Sweetie," as Jessie called Richard, had a ring of gold and diamonds designed for Jessie in the shape of the first bridge he built. It passed from Jessie to my grandmother to my mother to me. I have tried to identify the bridge. The Berry Bridge in Green County, Kentucky, built in 1908, is a possible candidate. In a photo celebrating the opening of the Berry Bridge, a mustached man wearing a suit and hat, seated near the front of the group in the middle of the picture, seventh from the left, bears a strong resemblance to R. N. Hudson, but I cannot be

The Spottsville Railroad Bridge in Henderson County, Kentucky, 1927

sure it is he.[22] Virginia's father's own careful hand identifies the "Green River Bridge, L. H. & St. L. Ry, Apr 1927," also called the Spottsville Railroad Bridge. It does not resemble the bridge on the ring, but he must have worked on it. It rotates one way to allow trains to pass over and rotates another way to disconnect itself from the main rail line to let barges pass.[23] The picture shows the bridge fully open. Originally built in 1888, after R. N. Hudson arrived in Kentucky, it was reconstructed in 1926 for the Louisville and Nashville railroad.[24] Surely Virginia's father was involved with the construction of the 1888 railroad bridge at Spottsville as well as the 1926 reconstruction.

Jessie delighted in making scrapbooks and took pride in collecting records of her husband's accomplishments. They tell something about his travels and hint at what Virginia was doing. I have a tattered book page that Jessie signed in Clifton Forge, Virginia, on July 27, 1911. That lone page tells that Jessie or the whole family must have passed time in Clifton Forge, a railroad hub since the late nineteenth century. Richard N. Hudson probably worked on the expanding C&O before and after 1911. Virginia would have turned seventeen by 1911, and she would have already eloped and been arrested by the constable. Perhaps she too spent time in Clifton Forge that summer?

My family and I rode over the C&O tracks and through Clifton Forge many times and on to Ashland, in eastern Kentucky, where we changed trains in the middle of the night to proceed on to Louisville. My mother frequently told of a conductor who called out, "Get out, all you hicks, get out." I assume the passengers who remained on the train were continuing to Ohio while we "hicks" were going to Kentucky. I wonder if my mother ever informed the conductor that the grandfather of one "hick" whom he shooed out in the night helped build the railroad.

The railroad connected Virginia and her family to people in high circles. In January 1915, R. N. Hudson was elected president of the L. H. & St. L. Railway.[25] The family moved from Cloverport, Jessie's hometown, to Versailles and then to Louisville after Hudson accepted the position as president. R. N. Hudson figures among the "prominent Louisvillians" in a 1916 press book, which records a residence in Versailles, Kentucky, and an apartment in Louisville at the Weissinger-Gaulbert building at Third and Broadway.[26] A photo captures R. N. Hudson standing to the far right of an L. H. & St. L. locomotive. Travel on the rails often took place in Virginia's father's private car, number 100, which unfortunately does not appear in any photos I have. The style of living it represented faded after R. N. Hudson's death, but nostalgic recollections drifted into conversations for many years.

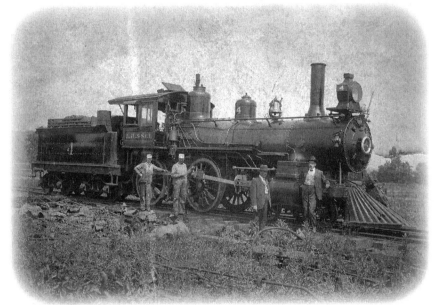

R. N. Hudson (far right) with L. H. & St. L. locomotive number 4, undated

Family members gathered in Cloverport for decades. My auntie Ann's diary for the late 1930s records numerous weekend visits there. Virginia spent time in Cloverport, my great-grandfather and his sisters owned property there, and Jessie had numerous family members living in the area. The Hudson family burial plots are located just outside the town. For my auntie Ann, burial in Cloverport meant reunion with her beloved mother and grandfather. In November 2008, Edward and I with close friends accompanied Auntie to her final resting place, making sure that she got to Cloverport, as she often requested, to be near her mother.

R. N. Hudson (second from right) with other men at the work yard for the L. H. & St. L. railway in Cloverport, Kentucky, undated	*R. N. Hudson (front row, center) with other men at the work yard for the L. H. & St. L. railway in Cloverport, Kentucky, undated*

Work yards for the L. H. & St. L. were located in Cloverport and then an important port city on the Ohio River. Photos show the work sites of the railroad and reveal my great-grandfather's willingness to work alongside his men, a character trait he imparted to his daughter, who chipped in to help whenever necessary.

My great-grandfather's contribution to railroad technology saved Auntie's life during one family emergency. Sometime after 1920, the year my auntie Ann was born, a chicken bone lodged in her throat, and my great-grandfather sped as fast as possible on the rail cart to fetch the nearest doctor and bring him back to remove it. My grandmother wrote of Ann's problems with

R. N. Hudson (left) with the first successful gas railcar in Cloverport, Kentucky, 1901

swallowing even as a baby, and the damage done by the chicken bone certainly did not help that. My great-grandfather's note attached to the photo states that this was the first successful gas railcar.[27] He assembled it at Cloverport, and it was photographed in 1901 near Cloverport by representatives from Fairbanks Morse and Company, at one time the largest manufacturer in the United States.[28]

At some point the family acquired an automobile that looks like an early pickup truck. The vehicle, nicknamed "Ida Red," centers an undated photograph from Cloverport. William, who worked for the family for thirty-five years, sits on the running board with a dog on either side.

William sitting on the running board of the "Ida Red," an early pickup truck, with a dog on either side, undated

Virginia's father worked with wealthy and powerful people for business dealings. One of those, James Ben Ali Haggin (1822–1914), attorney, rancher, investor, and horseman, was a native of Kentucky whose second wife lived in Versailles.[29] Connections from a small Kentucky town spread far outward. A letter that Richard wrote to Jessie on December 19, 1906, from the Waldorf-Astoria in New York, when he was general manager of the Louisville and Atlantic Railroad, reports that he met with Mr. Haggin and Mr. Choate, who had brought an automobile to New York from Connecticut.[30]

R. N. Hudson added that he spoke with former president Grover Cleveland, then residing in Princeton, New Jersey, after his second term (1893–1897). The promoters wanted to discuss a trolley deal and sought to have my great-grandfather influence Mr. Haggin. Their acquaintance was rooted in Kentucky and probably right in Versailles. Mr. Haggin made a fortune in copper and gold in California. In 1897, at the age of seventy-four, the multimillionaire Haggin married Margaret Pearl Voorhies, the twenty-eight-year-old niece of his former wife. Just prior to his marriage in Versailles, Haggin purchased a breeding farm for thoroughbred horses, Elmendorf Farm in Lexington. Around the time of my great-grandfather's 1906 letter, the Haggins were living in the Bluegrass and New York.[31] Mrs. Haggin gave a tract of land for Margaret College in Versailles, later Margaret Hall School,[32] which my grandmother and I both attended. Mrs. Haggin appears in *O Ye Jigs and Juleps!* under a different name, so my grandmother clearly knew Mrs. Haggin and one of her relatives.

Virginia's family enjoyed great respect from her father's prestige and character. Sometime after 1915 and before 1923, my great-grandfather had a country home built above a bend overlooking the Ohio River, near Cloverport (Breckenridge County) but in neighboring Hancock County. An undated story reprinted from the *Hawesville Clarion* reported that R. N. Hudson, president of the L. H. & St. L., would be building a home in upper Hancock County, east of the Federal Highway. The author praised my great-grandfather, in particular for placing a private car at the disposal of an ill person from Hawesville, Dorsey Powers, who needed to be taken to Cincinnati.[33] A different undated article reported that R. N. Hudson was "building a private airplane landing at his country home near Cloverport." The field was located on his several hundred acres, between the home and Cliff Lake Country Club, and was marked with a white canvas cross to make it visible to aviators. Among the expected guests was Harold J. Gates, for whom the field was named. Mr. Gates, a neighbor in St. James Court, was then touring the United States and Canada in his Ryan monoplane, "a sister to the Spirit of St. Louis," Charles Lindbergh's plane. A dated article, February 22, 1935, in the *Hancock Clarion* described the

scenic beauty of US Highway 60 from Breckinridge to Davies County. The author mentioned "a beautiful little country home nestled on the bank of the Ohio River" and observed that its owner Mr. Hudson had "an eye for the beauties of nature by the spot" he chose.[34]

The pictures I have from the country home date from 1823 to 1928. They show R. N. Hudson; Jessie; Virginia; his granddaughters, Virginia and Ann; Sallie, William;

Jessie Gregory Hudson and R. N. Hudson, 1910

the dogs, Bond and Billy; and many scenes of the house, the river, and the railroad tracks. One photo of Jessie and R. N. Hudson together dates from 1910. The open flat expanse around them would indicate that it not was taken in Louisville but in Cloverport or perhaps in Versailles. Jessie appears to be wearing a high coif without a hat on this sunny day.

Virginia wrote about spending an entire summer in Cloverport in 1922 and teaching Sunday school there. Her absence from Louisville surely relates to the divorce from Kirtley. She also recounted to her Louisville Sunday school class that she used to drive down routinely to help prepare the house for the annual visit of her father's friends during the autumn hunting season (*Close Your Eyes*, 83–84).

R. N. Hudson with two dogs, undated

Bond and Billy appear in numerous pictures, including several where the dogs, with noses to the ground, are tracking the site where Thomas Lincoln, father of Abraham, and his family stayed before crossing the river to Indiana in 1816. In the picture shown on page 17, the dogs flank R. N. Hudson.

My great-grandfather's love for dogs is evident from the praises he gave the dog Daniel in an obituary published in 1900 and from the many photos from Cloverport that include the dogs or picture them alone.

About one month ago there departed from this community a dog of remarkable ancestry. He was possessed of wonderful vivacity and looked upon by his associates as the King of all dogs. His name was Daniel which indeed was very appropriate. As a bird dog in the field he had few equals. In color he was white with pretty black spots covering his body … When this canine died there were none left in this country to fill his place.[35]

Virginia Cleveland and Ann Cleveland, holding a small dog, probably summer 1923

These photos show my mother holding a puppy or a small dog, perhaps a baby Doberman or even a miniature pinscher, just like Mia, the dog my daughter, Kathleen, chose for our family. One snapshot pictures Virginia and Ann in August 1923 with their grandfather holding the reins of a pony.

Virginia Cleveland and Ann Cleveland riding a pony while their grandfather R. N. Hudson holds the reins, August 1923

Family members used the 1929 pass pictured below for travel on the L. H. & St. L. In 1929, the L. H. & St. L. was consolidated with the L & N, and my great-grandfather became staff officer for operation of the L & N. R. N. Hudson appears in his new role standing with others before the number 359 railroad car of the L & N railroad. In 1932, he assumed the additional position of president and general manager of the Carrollton Railroad.

1929 L. H. & St. L. pass for family members of R. N. Hudson

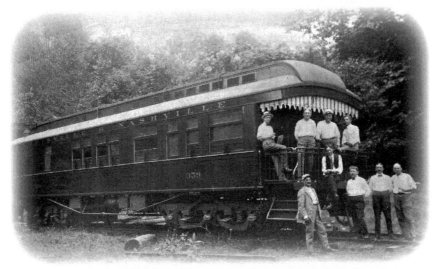

R. N. Hudson (second from right) and others with the
number 359 car of the L & N railroad

My great-grandfather's 1936 diary, the only one I have of his, records days spent in Louisville, meetings with Carrollton and with Kentucky Elevator, for which he served on the board, and other events. A member of Louisville's prestigious Pendennis Club, which opened in December 1928, R. N. Hudson signed his last check there on December 19, 1936, for the Pendennis luncheon: crabmeat cocktail, roast beef, iced tea, and charlotte russe, all for eighty cents, including the service charge.[36]

In late January 1937, the Ohio River overflowed its banks in several states and inundated about 70 percent of Louisville.[37] Auntie Ann's diary provides a brief day-by-day account. R. N. Hudson fell ill sometime earlier in January or in late December. As the flood worsened, so did his condition. He was brought by ambulance to higher ground, his daughter's home at 1439 St. James Court, on January 23, 1937. On the following day, the lights and water went off in the townhouse. The National Guard had been called into Hancock County, as into Jefferson County (Louisville) and numerous other places along the river. The streets of Louisville became impassable for days; the waters reached thirty feet above flood level, and 175,000 people were evacuated. Highway 60 from Louisville to Cloverport and beyond was submerged. The destruction must have devastated my great-grandfather, who had dedicated most of his life to building bridges, roads, and railways along and across the Ohio River. He passed away on January 25, 1937. Sadness enveloped the townhouse where his daughter and family then resided; his body had to remain there until the floodwaters subsided. By January 30, visitors reached Louisville from Woodford County. On the thirty-first, Pearson's Funeral Home came with a casket and took my great-grandfather to the funeral parlor. On February 10, Mr. Smith, president of the L & N railroad, provided his private car for the trip to Cloverport. Richard N. Hudson V was laid to rest on February 10, about three weeks after he died. The happy days at the country house were over.

How did the family go on in the midst of such tragedy? The heavy grief of my great-grandfather's death on auntie Ann's birthday weighed on her soul and the remembrance of her birthday for the rest of her life. Auntie's diary reveals Jessie's profound grief and disorientation. Jessie had her furniture moved to her daughter's house within a month, but she stayed periodically at the Brown Hotel. She also spent some time at the Mayflower Hotel. On July 5, 1938, she said that she was thinking about buying the house at 1453 St. James Court from Mr. Dabney (W. B. Dabney, an industrialist who made a fortune in paint). Three days later she bought the house for her daughter. By 1940 Jessie had moved to the Weisinger-Gaulbert, where she and Richard had lived. Kirtley did not get along well with either his mother-in-law or father-in-law. Auntie often recounted how "grandmother went to a hotel when she needed her 'peace and quiet.'" Jessie died five years after her husband, almost to the day, January 22, 1942. In 1946, the L & N sold R. N. Hudson's private railcar (no. 100) to a circus.[38]

Ten years after her father's death, Virginia wrote that he "represented the only tenderness I ever knew. With his passing my whole life changed; with his dying a part of myself died too. No sunlight has ever been as bright. Nothing has ever since seemed utterly worthwhile."[39] R. N. Hudson, known by all for his gracious manner and generosity, displayed a character very different from Kirtley Cleveland's.

Marriage and Remarriage to Kirtley S. Cleveland

My mother's notes for "Ah, Dear Readers" briefly cover Virginia's married life, stating that "when she was twenty, she married Kirtley S. Cleveland and bore him two daughters and a son." The newspaper wedding announcement states that Kirtley was a "junior member of the firm of Rout and Cleveland." The firm sold coal, grain, feed seeds, various construction materials, salt, and gasoline and had specialties in bluegrass seed, hemp, and wool. At some point Kirtley turned to training and owning thoroughbred horses, relying on some of his Woodford County friends as business partners.

Two photos show Virginia and Kirtley in Versailles sometime between 1913 and 1915, whether before or after their marriage,

I do not know. The lumber that appears behind Kirtley probably belonged to the company where he worked (photo, left), while Virginia, five feet nine inches tall, playfully extends her parasol. In the photo on the right, she stands at the corner of Elm and Main Streets, near the water tower.

*Virginia Cary Hudson Cleveland and
Kirtley S. Cleveland in Versailles,
Kentucky, between 1913 and 1915*

*Virginia Cary Hudson Cleveland
in Versailles, Kentucky,
between 1913 and 1915*

Their children were Virginia, my mother, born in November 1916; Ann, born in January 1920; and Richard, born in January 1930. The firstborn son, presumably named Kirtley, lived only a few days after birth. He died in Versailles on July 8, 1915. His loss pervades my grandmother's religious writings. A 1917 photograph captures Virginia at age twenty-two, holding my mother, six months old, on her lap. Eventually Kirtley and Virginia moved from Versailles to Louisville and settled in the neighborhood now known as Old Louisville. In 1930, they lived at 30 Reeser Street, and in October 1936, according to R. N. Hudson's diary, they moved to 1439 St. James Court, a townhouse a few doors from their future

Virginia Cary Hudson Cleveland, age twenty-two, 1917

home at 1453. The grand homes at St. James Court, many of them much larger than my grandparents', were constructed on the site of

Kirtley S. Cleveland on horseback with two thoroughbreds and two jockeys, date unknown, ca. 1940–1950

the Southern Exposition held in Louisville from 1883 to 1887. Prosperous industrialists proclaimed their wealth through the size, architectural design, and elegance of their homes. St. James Court, about two miles from Churchill Downs, offered my grandfather proximity to the track, a valuable convenience for a horseman's schedule and stream of visitors.

Kirtley excelled at choosing yearlings and training them for sale as two-year-olds. A photo shows "Mr. K. S." on horseback as he works with two thoroughbreds and jockeys. Pictured at the racetrack, probably in the 1950s, Kirtley wears binoculars, as he generally did at the track, and a summer hat. During the winter, he usually sported a navy-blue vest and suit coat and a dark hat. He wore bow ties more often than long ones. I remember picking out bow ties, always navy blue, for him at Christmas.

Virginia and Kirtley divorced sometime after the first two children were born. They later remarried. I suspect that a dispute over money provoked the conflict.

Kirtley S. Cleveland at the racetrack, 1950s

Memories haunted my mother all her life from the custody battle. "Granddaughter of Railroad President Abducted by Father," announced the leading headline on the *Courier Journal* (November 26, 1922). Ann's picture appeared under the photo, a sweet-looking two year-old wearing a ruffled bonnet. Auntie had no recollection of the kidnapping, she said, but my mother recalled that she and Ann were abducted and hidden in a closet in Versailles.

Both my grandparents demonstrated formidable character, the sort of people who stood out in any group, my father said. Kirtley displayed a magnetic charm and humor, but with that resided a stubborn harshness and grit. Carrie, a family household worker dear to my grandmother, considered "Mr. Cleveland" as "too old for Pretty," the affectionate name she gave my grandmother, and described him as filled with "vinegar and green persimmon juice."[40]

Tales of Kirtley's bold and outrageous acts abound. Even after a heart attack, he refused the doctor's order not to drive. In fact, after the physician told him to stay in the hospital and rest and under no circumstances drive, Kirtley promptly left his hospital bed, got into his car, and nearly ran over the startled doctor as he walked through the parking lot. In another case, Kirtley refused to pay what he considered an excessive bill for medical services. He instead instructed the physician how to receive even more than what he'd charged. Kirtley told him what day to go to Churchill Downs, what race and horse to bet on, and in what place (win, place, show). The physician collected as instructed and as promised. I remember my grandfather routinely charging through the Owner-Trainer Only entrance to Churchill Downs when he was in his sixties and seventies, if not before, refusing to show his owner-trainer pass and ushering family in with him. In his seventies, he griped, "I'm old, I'm tired, and I'm sick. Get out of my way." No one dared to stop him. When asked why he groused and grumbled, he replied with the number of his age: "I've got seventy-two reasons to feel poorly."

Beyond the Bluegrass: Virginia's Travels with Kirtley and the Horses

The adult Virginia traveled far beyond Highway 60 between Cloverport and Louisville, going to Cuba, Mexico, and Canada, where Kirtley raced his horses. My mother's notes for "Ah, Dear Readers" say that she was often asked, "What was Virginia doing during these years and what was her daughter doing?" The "Ah, Dear Readers" notes state simply that my grandmother "had a house full of roomers and she traveled with [her husband] in whatever area he happened to be racing."

Cuba

My grandmother put the French and Spanish she had studied to good use on the travels outside the country. When my mother and Auntie Ann were about eleven and eight years old, they accompanied their mother and father to Cuba. A souvenir photo postcard dates this stay in Cuba to early 1928.

Similar postcards from 1928 appear on eBay.[41] What was happening in Havana in 1928 that would explain the sale of these postcards from the same year? For one, the Sixth Pan American

Kirtley S. Cleveland (second from left) and three other men at the Tropical Garden in Havana, Cuba, 1928

Conference was held in Havana from January 16 to February 20, 1928. However, American tourism apparently reached a high level in 1928 for another reason, the Prohibition era in the United States (1920–1933). As Gustavo Pérez Firmat writes, "During the Roaring Twenties more than half a million Americans visited Cuba, since the passage of Prohibition in 1920 only enhanced Cuba's appeal as a licentious paradise … In the Prohibition Era, a vacation in Cuba was not a holiday but an 'alcoholiday,' as the *New Republic* phrased it in 1928. Cuba was now not only 'hot' but 'wet.'"[42] Moreover, American business money was pouring into Cuba, and American sugar mills were outpacing older Cuban mills.[43] Cuba in the 1920s "became a favorite destination for robber barons and bohemians," according to *Smithsonian Magazine*. "Scions like the Whitneys and the Biltmores, along with luminaries such as New York City mayor Jimmy 'Beau James' Walker, flocked to Cuba for winter bouts of gambling, horse racing, golfing and country-clubbing."[44] As Basile Woon wrote in 1928, Havana became "a second home for that section of the smart set which formerly spent its winters on the Riviera."[45] Another postcard pictures Al Capone at the Tropical Garden in 1930, between the mayor of Havana Julio Morales and a lawyer, J. Fritz Gordon.[46] The racetrack must have drawn American gangsters in addition to Capone, for Meyer Lanksy (1902–1983) reportedly had taken control of the track, Oriental Park, and the casino by 1937.[47]

Oriental Park, founded in 1915, operated during the winter months under the Havana-American Jockey Club. The racetrack attracted American owners of thoroughbreds and prepared future Hall of Fame jockeys.[48] It also hosted baseball games and in 1915 the heavyweight boxing championship between Jess Willard and Jack Johnson, an event that brought in $50,000 in bets.[49] Baseball figures such as the part owner of the New York Yankees, as well as the owner and the manager of the New York Giants, wintered in Havana. The revenues from tourism helped Cuban baseball to grow.[50] However, the boom of the 1920s was followed by economic decline and the overthrow of Cuba's president Gerardo Machado in 1933.[51]

My grandparents were not among the famous or the notorious

for whom the racetrack was a gathering place. The American ambassador's diary to Cuba shows that he participated in the world of Cuban horse racing and thus frequented places where my grandparents went, such as Oriental Park and dinners at the Jockey Club. Noble Brandon Judah, in his diary for the years 1928–1929, wrote that when he was there, the "people of the Island were prosperous and happy." He "left in the summer of 1929 before the beginning of the Great Depression."[52] Much social activity revolved around the racetrack, and my grandparents must have met him. Would that my grandmother's letters from this period remained! What priceless descriptions she must have written of the people she saw in Havana!

Reminiscing about the interruptions in her education because of my grandfather's travel with the horses, my mother recalled her experience at school in Cuba:

> The school day period of my life with my father's occupation as turf man was indeed colorful—I was in and out of any number of schools and in all parts of the country, even Cuba. This Cuban school I remember with great glee and immense joy! My sister and I just loved it! We boarded a small boat and crossed over to a small island. Mother could not understand our progress in this school. It was nil; we brought home nothing, and all our related news was of wonderful times. So, she went to school with us one day! Lo and behold they didn't speak any English!

I imagine that my grandmother found another school for Virginia and Ann, but I have no information about it. When Auntie passed eighty years old, she began to recount a memory from Cuba that we had not heard before. She said that she and my mother had waited on a street corner in Havana, perhaps after school, for my grandfather to pick them up but he had forgotten them. Darkness had descended, and Auntie had been terrified. She and my mother had not spoken Spanish, so they could only stand and wait for hours. My grandfather had arrived home without them and met my grandmother's dismay and anger. She had returned with him to the designated corner and picked up the girls. Auntie recalled that her mother had remained very angry for a long time.

Street view in Cuba, 1928

Virginia Cleveland (center) and Ann Cleveland (second from right) posing with three other girls (unidentified) in Cuba, 1928

Ann Cleveland (far left) and Virginia Cleveland (second from right) sitting with three other girls (unidentified) in Cuba, 1928

My photos offer peaceful glimpses of life in Cuba, such as the street corner, apparently on the other side of the wall from the house where the family was staying in Havana or perhaps in Marianao, a district of Havana where other family pictures were taken on the beach. A horse is tied up outside a store on a dirt street. Inside the wall around the house, Virginia and Ann pose with three other girls (unidentified) in two photos.

Some of the photos from Cuba capture moments of sisterly affection, like Virginia and Ann standing together on a rooftop terrace or hugging each other on the beach at Marianao. Juanita, who must have taken care of Virginia and Ann while their parents were at the racetrack, appears in a few photos. In the first, the three stand at the front gate

29

of the house. Second, on a cooler day Virginia and Ann wear coats. A third, a photo postcard, records Ann's eighth birthday, January 25, 1928; Virginia and Ann are wearing dress-up clothes.

Virginia Cleveland (left) and Ann Cleveland (right) on a rooftop terrace in Cuba, 1928

Ann Cleveland (left) and Virginia Cleveland (right) on the beach in Marianao, Cuba, 1928

Virginia Cleveland (left), Juanita (center), and Ann Cleveland (right) at the front gate of the house in Cuba, 1928

Virginia Cleveland (left), Juanita (center), and Ann Cleveland (right) beneath palm trees in Cuba, 1928

Virginia Cleveland (left), Juanita (center), and Ann Cleveland (right) on the beach in Marianao, Cuba, January 25, 1928

One picture, cut from a postcard, captures Virginia and Kirtley on the beach but dressed for a special occasion. Kirtley sports his usual bow tie and a straw hat, and Virginia wears high heels, a decorated hat, and a neck wrap.

Kirtley S. Cleveland and Virginia Cary Hudson Cleveland
on the beach in Cuba, probably 1928

Virginia and Ann do not seem to have gone to Oriental Park, although one dramatic story my mother told does place them there. According to my mother's recollection, she and Ann went to the track in Cuba one day with their mother, who had a sense of foreboding and thought she should keep the girls close at hand that day. One of Kirtley's horses was the hands-down favorite in a race. The crowd buzzed with the rumor that this horse's victory would be as sure a thing as a horse race ever gets. The bets, fast and heavy, rolled in. Just as the horses started onto the track, a late entry was announced, and a large, strong black horse pranced onto the track with the others. Virginia immediately ushered the girls out and away from the track as fast as she could and went straight to the American embassy. Someone from the embassy escorted them back to the house, and they arrived not long before a crowd rushed the gate pictured on page 30, carrying lit torches and yelling that my grandfather had fixed the race and betrayed them. My mother told me that she, her sister, and her mother exited the back just as the torch-carrying crowd crashed through the front gate to set fire to the house. They escaped the island in a boat that the embassy arranged. How or when my grandfather joined them, I do not know.

Virginia and her daughters apparently never returned to Cuba, but Kirtley certainly did. In a January 1930 letter to R. N. Hudson, Kirtley wrote from Havana about the birth of his son Richard in Kentucky. Kirtley pleaded to have the baby named for himself, but clearly to no avail. The letter's stationery comes from the Hotel Maison Royale in El Vedado, Havana. In the late 1920s, El Vedado flourished as Cubans thriving on high sugar prices built elaborate mansions and social clubs.[53] Unfortunately, I do not have other correspondence from this period. The photo of a school in New Orleans bears my grandmother's writing, "Ann's school." It may be that Virginia and the girls stayed in New Orleans for a time, while Kirtley was in Cuba. My grandmother must have written to her father and mother. It could be that those letters and many others perished in the 1952 fire at 1453 St. James Court.

Mexico

Just over a decade after Kirtley's 1930 letter, horse racing declined in the United States during World War II, and Kirtley took his horses to Mexico. My mother spoke of him racing and selling horses there both during and after the Depression. Agua Caliente, a track featured in the film *Seabiscuit*, opened in Tijuana in 1929. Unfortunately I have no photos or other records from there. Writing from Las Vegas in 1953, my grandmother mentioned buying a striking bracelet in Tijuana, but I have no more references to that city in her writings. I do have an envelope addressed to me from the Hotel Juarez, Mexico City, in 1951, but it was mailed from home in Louisville. Nonetheless, my mother handed on to me numerous colorful gifts from the Mexico travels—blankets, jackets, hats, jewelry and other bracelets, pottery, a colorful rug, and a photographic portrait of a famous bullfighter in an elaborately decorated jacket. My daughter and I share the jewelry, but I have given most of the other items to friends, as we have downsized our household possessions. A talk published in *Credos & Quips* provides a glimpse into my grandmother's experiences beyond the racetrack in Mexico. Always interested in religious traditions other than her own, she took the opportunity to attend Christmas Mass at the Metropolitan Cathedral in Mexico City. She wrote that all the benches had been removed and that the many people present were all on their knees. She was "sufficiently spiritually weak" that she needed to brace herself against a pillar. She remained for about an hour (*Credos & Quips*, 34).

This photo shows my grandfather and the winning horse Liberty Head at a track that must be the Hipódromo de las Américas, which opened in 1943 in Mexico City. Instrumental in funding the new track was Bruno Pagliai, the Italian industrialist.[54] My auntie Ann spoke of Mr. Pagliai coming to Kentucky for the derby and staying at St. James Court with the renowned bullfighter. She said that Mr. Pagliai enlisted my grandfather's expertise to buy horses and that he sent boxcars of them back to Mexico. My grandmother would have entertained the men during their stay in Kentucky, planned the meals, and

Kirtley S. Cleveland (far left) with the winning horse Liberty Head at the Hipódromo de las Américas, Mexico City

probably hired extra people to stage large dinner parties for horse-men and other guests. How I wish I had letters from this time!

Kirtley's success in Mexico appeared in a newspaper column sometime after 1951, while he was a partner and trainer with Clyde E. Buckley, a businessman from Lexington, Kentucky.[55] The story highlights the talent of my grandfather and Mr. Buckley at picking superior yearlings at Keeneland. My grandmother advised Kirtley and expressed strong opinions about the choices. Buckley purchased three successful yearlings in 1944; the horses were shipped with others to Mexico and trained there. The three—Plucky Flag, Transaction, and Martha Fly—won stakes races in Mexico. Plucky Flag captured the Mexican Triple Crown as a three-year-old. Market Level won the Spaulding Lowe Jenkins, a stakes race, at Laurel (Maryland) on October 20, 1951, and the winnings paid off a second mortgage on the house. W. R. Buster, director of the Kentucky Historical Society, informed my mother that the horse was bred by the famous King Ranch, Texas, and then sold as a "wean-ling" by Buster himself before be-ing purchased at the Keeneland sales.[56] My grandmother

Market Level, winner of the Spaulding Lowe Jenkins at Laurel (Maryland), 1951. Photo courtesy Joe Fleischer Studios, Baltimore, Maryland.

drew me pictures of Market Level and made me a blanket for the plush toy I named after the horse.

Canada

Besides Cuba and Mexico, Kirtley also took horses to Canada. Virginia wrote letters to her daughters in Louisville in 1938 and 1940 from Windsor, Ontario, the site of multiple racetracks. Ontario profited, as did Mexico and Cuba, from the years of Prohibition in the United States. Furthermore, the variety of tracks in a small area allowed horsemen the opportunity to test a horse's skills in multiple venues. In a 1946 letter written from Louisville, my grandmother informed my mother that Kirtley had invited "Don Carlos," a Canadian nightclub owner, to 1453 St. James Court. Another millionaire to entertain! In September 1952 letters from the Frontenac Arms Hotel in Toronto she mentioned Charles Hemstead (1892–1961), a prominent Toronto businessman and horseman, probably the Don Carlos of 1946. In 1952, Kirtley and Joe Rogers worked a horse on the Dufferin Park in Toronto to see if he could make the quick half-mile turns there before shipping him to Wheeling, West Virginia. Hemstead hosted an elegant dinner at his club and spoke of owning fifty-three mares and five studs. My grandmother described him as wearing "a solitaire as big as a nickel and a horse shoe stickpin three inches long of diamonds, about one and a half carats." Another evening Hemstead gave his wrestling tickets to my grandparents after they had spent the day at the races seated in the box of the Canadian distillery Seagram's chief, whose dealings with bootleggers are noted in recent publications about the Prohibition era.[57] My mother recalled that my grandfather obtained a concoction known as "Bell's Tonic" in Canada, a sort of energy drink that gave the horses more pep.[58] On days when she was tired, mother wished whimsically for a dash of Bell's Tonic. The Bell's Company (UK) website displays the current Bell's Tonic, available only for export.

Kirtley also took his horses to numerous tracks in the eastern half of the United States, including Churchill Downs and Miles Park in Kentucky; Beulah Park in Ohio; Delaware Park; Laurel Racecourse, near my family's home in Maryland; Waterford Park,

Wheeling Downs, and Shenandoah Downs in West Virginia; and Suffolk Downs in Massachusetts. Kirtley's horses were not famous. He excelled at identifying yearlings with good potential, training them, and selling them after they won claiming races. He earned respect as a trainer, and MacKenzie "Mack" Miller, Hall of Fame trainer, worked for Kirtley as an apprentice.[59]

Las Vegas

Virginia's letters record one visit to the West in September 1953, first to see a friend who had moved to San Diego from St. James Court and then to the colorful world of Las Vegas, during the short time that a racetrack operated there—the first and last racing season at Las Vegas Park. The park opened September 4, 1953, and stayed open only thirteen days. Those days apparently were not consecutive. Virginia wrote on October 6, about a month after the opening, "The horses are only running two days a week, Saturday and Sunday. The purses have been cut in half, and the stake races your father brought Buckley's horses to win have been called off." Another attempt at launching horse racing in Las Vegas also failed in the 1960s.[60]

Two eating places stand out among the vivid depictions of places, people, and happenings that my grandmother recorded. Perhaps some people would not have even passed through the doors, but the names of both drew her in: "Margie's Hells Bells Home Cooking" and "Horrible Herbert."

> Out in the desert near the talcum mines, I saw a shack, "Margie's Hells Bells Home Cooking." I never wanted a Kodak so badly. Margie is a good-looking old bat who must have been a knockout in her day. The sand and heat have hardened her feet until they look like hooves. Her hair short and tangled. A scarf is tied around a pleasing bosom and about her waist are two aprons. A narrow scant one about her backsides, exposing fiery red drawers, and a ruffled

one in front. Her shoulders are dimpled and her arms and legs deserving of any sculptor's notice. In the leather strap around her waist is a vicious looking knife. She whistles while she cooks, "Listen to the Mockingbird." That is because she says "she ain't never heard one." I just love Margie and her "Hells Bells" kitchen.

The name of the second eating place apparently expressed the owner's mood. "I went to a joint today called 'Horrible Herbert.' He curses all day long. When I ordered orange juice and said, 'That's all,' he told me, 'By God it'd better be. I'm damn well sweated out.'"

Another view of human experience beckoned when Virginia spotted a hitchhiker in pink boots walking in the intense desert heat.

Coming back [from the airport] I saw a cow-hand walking in the broiling sun. Stopped to offer him a ride. "Ride with you in that?" he asked me. "Sure," I told him. "I don't think it will blow up and I know I don't bite." So he got in and took off his shirt and pink boots. He introduced himself as Calamity Cal and insisted on shaking hands. "Why Calamity Cal?" I asked him. His father was a drunkard, his mother died when he was born, the orphanage burnt down, a son of a bitch took him home, he married the wrong woman, bank failure got his savings and foreclosed on his home, and his best friend rustled his cattle. He told me he could tell me more. Told him that was enough for any one man. Deer season begins Sunday (today) and he invited me up to his shack in Cherry Creek for venison spread. Said I didn't "seem like no woman, more like a man." When I put him out, I stopped by a truck. And it was painted "Big Sam hires anybody and pays nobody. A good bed and all you can eat four times a day."

Margie, Horrible Herbert, Calamity Cal, Big Sam, and his employees revealed the hardship of living and working in a desert mining and gambling town. As my grandmother described it, miners came out of gold, silver, talcum, and magnesium mines to brawl downtown and seek out the rooms for prostitution above the saloons and dance halls.

The Native Americans my grandmother saw in Las Vegas, most likely members of the Paiute tribe, revealed the poverty and suffering that had been inflicted by white settlers and railroad builders who forced the Paiutes to labor on their own land.[61] She observed them setting up stoves and cooking in the gutters. She admired them and painfully understood the distrust they showed her and the refusal of the older tribe members to converse with her. She compared the Paiutes to the wealthy showgoers and gamblers: "Their modesty and dignity far surpasses that of their white brother who considers himself so superior with his brazen and artificial way of life." I wonder how many people with lodging in glitzy Las Vegas hotels ventured into conversations with the Paiutes or Calamity Cal and Margie. My grandmother opened herself to the reality of life around her, observed it astutely, and recorded all that she could.

The wealthy occupied the hotel strip and spent time at the casinos and shows. A famous opera star, Lauritz Melchior, was staying with his wife at the same hotel as my grandparents. It was perhaps the Thunderbird, which is the logo on the one envelope I have postmarked from Las Vegas. It is one of a few letters I have that my grandmother wrote to my father. More often she added messages for him in letters that she addressed to my mother at our home in Maryland.

Melchior was performing at the more famous and elegant Sahara Hotel from September 20 to October 20 in 1953.[62] My grandmother noticed and described the minute details of his appearance, as she did with other people.

> I was going to tell you how Melchior was dressed
> for breakfast. He had on a white shirt and neatly

arranged tie. Over that was his silk pajama coat, unfastened. His pajamas were a fierce and startling yellow with designs of green cacti, brown jackasses, and red banjos. His pajama trousers were rolled up above his knees, showing his crooked, hairy legs, and on his feet were red toweling shoes. You know that fat-cheeked Santa Claus grin he gets on for his public? That is strictly a stage face. At the table he was as sullen and glum as he could be. Hoping that I become neither, I am, with love, Mother.[63]

My grandmother recorded other encounters with the Melchiors and took Lauritz to the races one day, telling him to bet on Little F, who was a sure winner that day. He gleefully collected the winnings from his ten-dollar bets and kissed her on the cheek. She was sure no one would believe this story, saying, "If I come back and say that Lauritz Melchior kissed me, people will think the older I get, the bigger liar I become."

Virginia found one Episcopal church in Las Vegas—probably Christ Church, founded in 1907, which sold its downtown church in 1954 and dedicated a new building in 1962.[64] She described it as "placed on the lot wrong. The front door, after you get in, is up by the organ, and the entrance is around back where you never see it." Her first visit attracted notice. "I went into the organ door within a few feet of the preacher who was in the middle of his sermon. There was dead silence. I was as big as the organ, and the wings on that white bird I have on my hat almost touched

Virginia in a large white hat in the 1950s

the rafters." Recall that Virginia without a hat or heels was five feet nine inches tall. She explained that the bird on her hat had shed feathers on the journey west. At San Juan Capistrano, famous for the return of the swallows there every year, she'd picked up feathers on the ground and sewed them to the bird, resulting in it gaining "much the proportions of an albino eagle." The startled preacher stopped his sermon and escorted her to the front bench. The ladies from the church received her happily and entertained her during her stay. In a later letter, she remarked that the assistant minister reminded her of a family friend named Harry.

> He is very young, and fat like Harry, and just as tall! He preaches just about how Harry would preach, and scratches his stomach while he sings. His sermon, in reality a defense of Las Vegas lawlessness, was something! The text was, "a decent but godless people." The self-righteous he blasted to hell.[65]

In T. S. Eliot's poem "The Rock," he speaks of a "decent godless people: / Their only monument the asphalt road / And a thousand lost golf balls."[66] An Internet search brings to light hundreds of places where preachers cite those words. I wish I could find a reflection on that text written in my grandmother's hand for the Louisville ladies. She certainly would agree with the Las Vegas preacher on blasting the self-righteous.

Virginia summed up her Las Vegas experience in a letter written on a Sunday, possibly October 4 or October 11, 1953. She listed the people she would miss. Apart from the few Episcopalians she'd met, the list was primarily working people she saw on a regular basis.

> Today the horse car will be ordered, and by Saturday or Sunday we should be home. I will miss the gaiety and open frankness of the Episcopalians, all so far from home. I will miss old Emmanuel, and the waitresses, and Janie Lee in the ladies lounge. I will miss the pretty woman who washed my hair. I will miss the policeman who waves to me when I pass. I will miss the nits and the sand, and believe

it or not, I will even miss the dice and wheels. I have never been anywhere, any time, that I have not found something to enjoy, and something in which there was sufficient good to always remember, plus, everywhere something, always to learn.[67]

Virginia came face-to-face with corruption in West Virginia, as she had in Cuba and undoubtedly in other places. Kirtley frequently took the horses to Wheeling Downs and to Waterford Park, constructed in 1950. On a summer trip in 1952, my grandmother Virginia was waiting in the heat of the car for the horses to arrive from Canada when a man kindly invited her to his air-conditioned office and had his butler serve her supper and a cool drink.[68] She entertained him with stories of Cloverport personalities. He "rocked" at tales of the spiritualist "Wicked Wick" and his boat, the *White Dove.* Her host kept a crystal ball himself in a carved case. He turned out to be "Big Bill" Lias (1900–1970), the West Virginia gangster who reportedly made his fortune in illegal alcohol sales during Prohibition and then in gambling afterward.[69] Lias bought Wheeling Downs in 1945. During the 1950s, he was frequently under investigation. My grandmother's letter reported, "He is a gangster and owes the gov't six million dollars. He is supposed to have poisoned his wife and had his sweetie's husband murdered. Everybody hates him and is scared to death of him."

Future encounters with the owner and his family were inevitable at a small racetrack. Mrs. Lias invited my grandparents to her birthday luncheon. Unfortunately I do not have a letter that describes it. In anticipation of attending, Virginia said that she "expected" her "poor mother's departed spirit to slap [her] out of the chair." The Liases' daughter was too young to buy her own pari-mutuel tickets. On Wednesday, August 27, 1952, she persuaded my grandmother to do her betting for her. The girl had a program in which her father had placed a check mark by his chosen winner in every race. I still have that very program. Virginia placed her own bets on the marked horses in seven races, but she had to leave the track before the eighth race. All seven won. She closed the letter with what may have been a riposte to her departed mother: "'Trust & Obey, and the Lord will provide,' and the Good Book doesn't say one damn thing about from what source. I miss you. Love, Mother."

On one stay in Wheeling, my grandmother observed that a priest frequented a place called the Cricket Club. She reported, "He always ordered two cocktails to accompany a four dollar steak. After consuming the former and devouring the latter, he would disappear into the chuck-a-luck room to test the power of holiness against the chances of evil." (Chuck-a-luck, the name of a dice game, serves here as a broad term for gambling.) As her farewell to Wheeling on that 1952 trip, Virginia drew a picture of the priest, folded it, and pinned it to his steering wheel. What did she draw?

> The picture was a big old fat priest, with a cross around his neck and a prayer book in one hand marked "Novenas." He was running for his life, or rather his salvation. Dragging him by his other hand was an angel, jet propelled, going at such a rate that smoke was issuing from his tail hole. His halo was tilted sideways, and his crown was down over one eye. His big bare toes were spread, and his robe was whipped up around his potbelly. Behind these two was the devil, tail straight up in the air, spitting flame. Down the road from this racing trio was St. Peter, standing at the wide-open gates of heaven. Near the entrance was the Pope sitting on his dais, with lace drawers showing beneath his surplice, waving his arms and shouting, "Come on, brother."[70]

Under this picture that my grandmother took hours to draw, she wrote, "I hope you made it." Wheeling was a frequent stop on my family's journey by car from Washington, DC, to Louisville, and I recall that we saw my grandfather there on some trips. We dined at the Cricket Club, where I delighted in the Shirley Temple cocktails with little paper umbrellas and extra maraschino cherries. Years after those trips, I asked my father about another memory of the Cricket Club, that the parking lot out front was always jammed with cars but the restaurant where we ate never seemed to be filled. He laughed and told me that the area of the club on the other side of the dining room was where the gambling took place.

An education at the racetrack

I was beginning my first year of school in Landover Hills, Maryland, when my grandparents stayed in Las Vegas. What a time I missed! My memories from the racetracks I visited often merge somewhat indistinguishably. I went to Churchill Downs many times, but I do not remember whether my grandmother accompanied us or not. I suspect that most of my recollections date from after her passing. I vividly remember attending the Keeneland sales, near Lexington, Kentucky, and watching the horses being brought out. The forceful cadence of the auctioneer's voice overrode the crowd noises with the call for bids, such as, "Three, three, three thousand, do I hear three thousand? Bid for three. Do I hear four thousand? Bid for four. Do I hear five? Four, four, four thousand, do I hear four, four, four, going for four thousand. Going, going, gone for four thousand." And then he slammed the gavel, finalizing the sale. Current prices are much higher, the venue is more elegant, and electronic number boards assist attendees with following the lengthy numbers being called at a near-breathless pace. At the age of five, caught up in the mesmerizing chant and full of mischief, I raised my hand, the sign of a bid, and the auctioneer recognized me. Auntie gasped in shock, but another bidder quickly raised my bet, thank heavens.[71] I wrote to Auntie from Revere, Massachusetts—home to Suffolk Downs—on April 25, 1955. I was missing school for the races! That trip remains a prized memory. I snuck into the barn area once with my grandfather and father and then to a morning workout. I was small enough to disappear when I walked between them. My father and I practiced taking steps together in time—a challenge for his six-feet-two-inch frame and my not-quite-eight-year-old legs. I witnessed the mystique of horses pounding against the pace of stopwatches in the dark before dawn. The empty stands echoed the sounds of hooves and fast-breathing animals. The exact whereabouts of that track have faded in my mind, but I commented to Auntie about Revere, "It's against the law up here for children to go to the racetrack. Feed Little F sugar most every morning myself." My recollection of an early morning at the racetrack very probably comes from Suffolk Downs then, about half an hour from where I live now in Cambridge, Massachusetts. I do remember visiting Paul Revere's house in Boston and the USS *Constitution* in addition to Suffolk Downs, so I imagine that I spent some time doing historical sightseeing in the Bay State.

In stark contrast to Churchill Downs, Suffolk Downs did not allow me to place bets. In Kentucky, I would be given two dollars for the day, and I would cautiously choose the favorites to show (finish third or better) in order to make small gains of twenty or forty cents and come out as the day's only winner. Once I was tall enough to see over the betting window, I placed some bets myself (not illegal in Kentucky). But most of the time, I kept busy searching for pari-mutuel tickets that might have been discarded in error. I put them in a shopping bag and sorted through to look for possible hidden treasure. The pari-mutuel system was second nature to me, so much so that I explained it complete with sample discarded tickets to my kindergarten class, much to the scandal of the teacher, a strict Presbyterian who objected to gambling and told my mother I was corrupting the other children. Later, when I was in fifth grade, my teacher gave the sternest warning ever about my attendance at the races. She scolded my mother for taking me out of school to go to the Kentucky Derby, and what is more, she told my mother that I was never going to like school. On the contrary, I chose a career that has kept me happily in school for sixty-three years, from my days as a student to those as a professor. When I received my first letter of appointment from Harvard, my mother framed it, hung it in the living room in Pompano Beach, did a "hillbilly hop" around the room and said, "Ta-da, Mrs. X! She's teaching at Harvard!" Her eyes welled with tears because her mother could not share the pride she felt.

I had my favorite horses, and indeed Little F, a beautiful gray horse, was one of them, as was Little Auntie, sold in 1963 at Miles Park.[72] Little F is pictured in the winner's circle at Churchill Downs in 1953 (p. 46). Another photo where Little F poses in the winner's circle was snapped at Waterford Park the same year. Aboard the gray filly is none other than Bill Hartack, the Hall of Fame jockey. Hartack's first victory came on October 14, 1952, at Waterford Park. By the 1953 season, Hartack had won 350 races. One of those occurred on July 8, 1953, the occasion for this photo. Hartack quickly moved up in the racing world, winning the Kentucky Derby five times, the Preakness Stakes three times, and the Belmont Stakes once.[73] He and the famous Eddie Arcaro rode for Kirtley S. Cleveland early in their careers. One of the two eventually remarked to my grandfather, "I don't need to ride your cheap horses anymore, Mr. Cleveland." Unfortunately, pictures of them aboard Kirtley's horses were destroyed in a basement flood in my home. During visits for the derby in the spring, we frequently went to Churchill Downs with my grandfather. I remember visiting the stables to feed sugar or carrots to the horses. Once inside the track, perched atop a folding chair in the grandstand, I experienced the thrill of watching the horses race, cheering on whichever horse my mother or I had chosen. I remember waiting for my grandfather's final decision on each race. He studied the *Daily Telegraph* (racing form) meticulously, but he never made a decision until he had seen the horse's legs in the saddling paddock or as it made the first steps into the open from the passage under the stands. In the 1950s his seats at Churchill Downs were located where the horses first step out from the passageway, so he could see them from just above. Then he would place his bet hurriedly in the few minutes remaining. When present, my father would make his way quickly through the crowd, his tall frame clearly visible, to the betting window with Kirtley's wagers. The photo on page 47 shows Kirtley outside Churchill Downs on May 8, 1941, studying a program, and another man with the *Daily*

*Little F in the winner's circle at Churchill Downs with
Virginia Cleveland Mayne, Ann Cleveland, and Beverly
Mayne (left) and Kirtley S. Cleveland (right), 1953*

*Little F in the winner's circle at Waterford Park with
Bill Hartack aboard and Kirtley S. Cleveland and
Virginia Cary Hudson Cleveland, July 8, 1953*

Telegraph, perhaps before the gates opened for the day. Behind them, under the arches, is the saddling paddock.

At the entrance to the track on busy days, I saw the faces of poverty and disability in young men who were probably war veterans. Not long ago I found Internet postings from people my age who advocate now for veterans returning from recent wars and who remember painfully the

Kirtley S. Cleveland reading the day's program outside Churchill Downs, May 8, 1941

veterans selling pencils in the 1950s. The young men sat on limbs that stopped at the knees, pant legs folded under their thighs, and they appealed to racegoers to buy pencils at a nickel apiece. I often brought nickels and chose pencils from the neatly arranged collections stacked in cigar boxes. They leaned over to reach the boxes—at risk of falling, I thought—and those who could extended a hand to offer me the pencils. I think that some had lost arms. I have not forgotten their faces, their missing limbs, or their sad eyes.

The poor and disabled at the entrance to the track, outside an edifice built from money and power, bespoke abuse and neglect by society. Similarly, the mistreatment of racehorses stands out in stark contrast to the majestic beauty of proud animals racing neck and neck around the track on slender, graceful legs. Around the horses' stately elegance and remarkable beauty spins a human circle of gambling and corruption. In recent years journalists have uncovered twenty-first-century roads to winning races that involve despicable abuse of animals. Virginia's letters to my mother tell about the dark side of racing—stable fires suspected as arson, jockeys pushing each other off their horses and over the track rail, and a horse abandoned to die because the van was moving on to another track. In response to this last injustice, my grandmother wrapped the horse in cloths spread with Vicks salve, administered appropriate doses of quinine with the help of a local pharmacist, and nursed it back to health. The owner sent my grandmother a case of stewed tomatoes to thank her for saving a horse he had left for dead.

At Home in Louisville

But what did Virginia do when she was at 1453 St. James Court and not traveling? The inside flap of the cover for *Close Your Eyes When Praying* claims that "Mrs. Hudson was a grandmother and widow earning a precarious living as proprietress of a Louisville, Kentucky boarding house." My mother was shocked by the errors in the publisher's wording. She had not seen or approved the inside cover before publication. My grandmother was never Mrs. Hudson, and she was never a widow. My grandfather outlived her by eleven years. And her home was not a boardinghouse. For several years after her daughters were grown, she accepted two roomers at a time. As far as I know, they occupied the two second-floor rooms on either side of the back staircase. They paid for a room but not board—that is, daily meals. Those misconceptions circulated in numerous reviews of the books.

In fact, the house was often filled with visitors. Virginia entertained countless houseguests, especially at Derby and during racing season. She kept up with costs and repairs on the big house and cleaned the house with the help of one or more workers. She addressed women's groups on topics of religion, played a role in managing the St. James Court Association for around fifteen years, and suffered debilitating and constant pain from kidney stones. My mother moved to Washington, DC, in 1946. The stream of letters I have begins then and illuminates what went on in the house, in St. James Court, and on the frequent journeys with the horses.

Horse racing had many ups and downs. My grandfather lost everything more than once, suffering two devastating stable fires and a foreclosure on more than twenty houses he was renovating and renting when the banks closed at the Depression. The large house at St. James Court was expensive to keep up and to heat. Rent from the roomers allowed for predictable income and for the house to be occupied steadily during the many travels my grandfather and my grandmother undertook.

Visitors flowed into the house at 1453 St. James Court during racing season, when my grandparents remained in Louisville. Bruno Pagliai and Charles Hemstead were perhaps the most famous but far from the only guests. Alterations to the house enclosed the two side porches in front so that extra guests could be accommodated.[74] The original house was built about 1907 and designed by well-known architect George Tachau. David Dominé features it in *Old Louisville: Exuberant, Elegant, and Alive.*[75] When I discovered it as the *Courier Journal* Home of the Week (February 14, 2013), magnificently renovated and furnished by the current owners, I could at last see inside again and confirm the memories of its rooms that I have held since childhood.

The description of 1453 St. James Court in *Old Louisville* states that "evidence suggests that the three large arches in the façade were originally open."[76] Letters from my grandmother reveal details about alterations. A letter of May 29, 1946, reports that the "porch rooms

are done." My grandmother did have the two porches to the left and right enclosed to make additional rooms.[77] Two photos from 1946 show the side porches enclosed but the center still open.

Virginia Hudson Cleveland, Virginia Cleveland, and Kirtley Cleveland in the center doorway of the house at 1453 St. James Court, 1946

Ann Cleveland in front of the center doorway of the house at 1453 St. James Court, 1946

One letter written by my grandmother to my mother before I was born assured her that there was plenty of room for her to come with friends from Washington, DC—nine bedrooms, one rollaway bed, one cot, one cradle, and two couches.[78] The same year, my grandmother wrote, "The races are on, with the usual attending torrent of company dropping in. Mob coming for Derby." She complained, "Your father had two hoodlums visit him for the Derby. Kansas City streetcar motormen," and she observed, "Last Derby we had a house full of millionaires. This year I had one full of bums."[79] Virginia's letters to her daughter include reports on the status of my grandfather's Derby tickets. Long before the race, my grandmother dealt with various bids for individual tickets from the block that Kirtley owned, complaints about their location, and haggling over the price. In a sense, she managed the part of his business that touched home, from Derby tickets to communication with bookies.

Virginia got the idea to rent rooms during Derby weekend from a neighbor who successfully did the same. She wrote about eventual longer-term renting to two teachers, and she described the applicants for rooms—those she accepted and those she rejected. She recounted the roomers' adventures with characteristic wit and compassion. I remember fondly one of the roomers, Fortuna Gordon, who was a professor at the University of Louisville. I listened with fascination as she read to me and told me about her journeys and the languages she spoke. We were honored by her presence while she stayed. I suspect that her warmth and erudition must have had some influence on my career path.

When we arrived at my grandmother's home, the house seemed to open its arches to embrace me. I recall running as fast as I could up the walkway to greet Auntie and my grandmother when we reached Louisville after the eighteen-hour car trip from Maryland. Once I tripped on the steps at the street side of the walk, fell just in front of Auntie, and pierced my lip with my lower front teeth. I still have a small scar from the stitches. I visited St. James Court two to three times per year from the time of my baptism in Kentucky in 1947 until the sale of the house in 1957 after my grandmother's death in 1954. I remember the lovely high staircase that drew my eyes and my feet upward, and I recall the lovely fountain, the hexagonal-blocked sidewalks in the neighborhood, the sheltering trees of Central Park, and the lasting sweet odor of bourbon mash in the air. The big house was filled with corners to explore, a rear staircase to climb, and enigmatic areas from the coal bin in the cellar to the attic.

Virginia Cleveland (daughter) before the original fountain at St. James Court, before 1946

The mysterious dark attic was adjacent to the third-floor rooms where my auntie Ann resided at the top of the rear staircase. The stairs resounded with the clack of Auntie's high heels when she went up and down to work each day. I stayed up on the third floor during our visits to Louisville, but I did not know how to reach the attic. Auntie welcomed me with new toys and allowed me to do things my parents did not permit, such as stenciling Christmas designs on the windows with Glass Wax, wearing lipstick and powdering my nose, giggling past my bedtime, or rising extra early to play, especially at Christmastime. At three and a half, I beat a tom-tom around the house at four in the morning and wore an "Indian suit" complete with feather headdress.

Beverly Mayne in Kentucky at Christmas, 1950

When I was a bit older, my mother and grandmother took me in May 1952 to explore the attic. As mother wrote,

So much went on upon any and every visit home that our time was really so limited to do as we pleased. But this visit we finally found the time to climb to the third floor and into the old attic. We planned to bring downstairs the many things that sat in the old trunks, for my grandmother "kept things." Some people do "keep things." I'm one of this variety. Now my grandmother was always immaculate, everything about her, and when she put something away, it was indeed a ritual. She used tons of tissue paper, endless boxes, miles of string and her knots! Even Harry Houdini could not untie that which she wrapped. Each article was fixed, as if, in those days it might be going to China. The old diaries, ancient books and the like Virginia's daughter was just dying to copy.

Mother, Beverly, and I went up the steps to the third floor attic. The dust and the dirt were thick. Dark as midnight. We ran an extension cord out thru the doorway so that we might see. Finally, after much difficulty, the top of one of the old trunks was opened. Yes, Grandmother had surely tended to the putting away of many articles in this old trunk. Lying on top was a very old dress amid a mountain of tissue paper. We brought it out to the light and unfolded it. Out came the longed for old books and diaries, prayer books, old records, old newspaper clippings, hymnals. Then with much care we lifted out Grandmother's scrapbook. It was "fat" with keepsakes and memories which had been stored between its covers. Here we found old letters, records, ancient newspaper clippings, and the like. I picked up lined papers, yellow with age, but in beautiful condition, and I read "An Afternoon's Stroll."[80] We read on and on. I was delighted! Enchanted! Mother and I laughed and laughed, and she told me she wrote them in her tenth and eleventh year. "Mother we must take them downstairs and copy them for Beverly," I said. "They are the cutest little pieces I have ever heard." This was my immediate request. She agreed to help me copy them. We closed the lid of the old trunk, walked down the steps carrying the old dress, several small books, and Grandmother's scrapbook. We were filthy dirty.

The remaining days of my visit were spent in copying the essays on my mother's portable typewriter which had a red ribbon in it. On the day I left Kentucky to return to Maryland, I carefully put the essays back into the scrapbook, closed its covers, walked back to the third floor, lifted the lid of the old trunk, and put the rose covered keepsakes safely away. What a mistake!

A letter from my grandmother about the October 1952 fire opens with the news that the men are working in the rafters of the third floor. She planned "a large dormer window in front of the roof, which [would] give the house the appearance of being a third story structure, which you could not distinguish before." In addition there would be "two windows in Ann's [my auntie's] room which face west, as well as two in the other room."[81] The photos below show the house with the center vestibule enclosed and the dormers and windows on the third floor.

1453 St. James Court, 1989

A caretaker, a fountain, and flat tires: Managing St. James Court

Despite her many travels, my grandmother accepted a leading role in her community: serving on the St. James Court Association for

The St. James Court fountain, 1995. Photo by the author.

about fifteen years, from her election as secretary and treasurer in 1939 to her years as president. The association operated the property at St. James Court, which was the private land of the homeowners. On a Sunday in 1946, she wrote, "This Thursday I resign as President of St. James Ct. Ass'n. Eight years I have wrestled with lawn mowers and a fountain." However, in a letter from that Thursday she reported, "The ladies of the St. James Court Ass'n. have come and gone. One burst into tears over my resignation. Result another term."[82]

As soon as Virginia took office in 1939 after the March 23 annual meeting, she saw to it that the caretaker's wage was raised— in fact, quadrupled. The St. James Court record states that March 31 marked the end of his two-dollar-per-week wage and April 7 the beginning of his eight-dollar weekly wage. Sadly the caretaker, Melvin Sanders, fell ill and passed away the following year. My grandmother entered an obituary for Melvin, an employee of thirty years, into the record.

> Melvin Sanders, caretaker of St. James Court and personal servant of some of the Court's first residents, died the first day of February 1940 at his house on

Oldham Street after prolonged and intense suffering due to an incurable malady. Melvin loved St. James Court and many of its people. In every newcomer, of whom I am one, he felt and showed a kindly and cooperative interest. Any compliment in conjunction with the Court cast over his aging features a warm glow of personal satisfaction. Even the Son of God saw fit to pause in his limited ministry to render praiseworthy recognition on behalf of "a good and faithful servant."

Virginia and Mrs. Joyes (previous president of the association) officially engaged George Hampton, Melvin's choice, to become the permanent caretaker of St. James Court after Melvin's death. Mrs. Joyes had aroused the ire of many in Louisville when she'd had barbed wire strands placed around the hedge rows and around the fountain at St. James Court. In the newspaper article "'Ouch Hedge' Stirs Row," Mrs. Joyes defended her decision and said that she had discussed it with police and that she also had secured legal advice that the association was within its rights to place the barbed wire around the hedges. Mrs. Joyes further stated that the decision was not unfair to children who did not live in the court, because they had free access to the nearby Central Park. My grandmother was to establish a different tone in her administration.

The fountain, topped by a statue of a graceful lady, was and is the centerpiece of St. James Court. For many years its condition was poor and even perilous. Virginia feared that crumbling pieces would injure someone, especially a child, and she did her utmost to persuade the residents to contribute to its repair. Her letters mention efforts to raise funds from the membership so that repairs could be done. On October 19, 1951, she wrote, "Tomorrow night the members of St. James Court Association meet here at eight o'clock. The fountain is going to cost $750. I want it repaired or taken down, and I don't mean maybe. It is not going to stand there and fall down and go to pot!" Then on March 2, 1952, my grandmother sent my mother news that quavered with an ironic tragedy that reinforced her fears about the fountain: "The man who is to fix the fountain warned me again and again about it being in condition to fall on somebody's child. It is pathetically tragic that a few days ago a boiler fell from a scaffold in his own shop and crushed to death his own 17 year-old son. Life surely batters some of us without mercy and without seeming justice." The man fixing the fountain and my grandmother had both suffered the loss of a child, and both did their utmost to prevent another senseless death. Another letter from 1952 reports that a resident of St. James Court had the fountain propped up at his own expense and anonymously. Perhaps he hired the man to fix it. By 1972 the lady and the fountain were crumbling. When the lady was removed from the top for shipping and recasting, she broke into pieces. As Joan Riehm wrote in the *Courier Journal*, "So last December [1972], the fountain was dismantled for shipment to Michigan, where it could be recast into time-resistant bronze. But the maiden didn't make the trip, and she won't be seen again."[83]

However, another statue was in place atop the fountain by 1975, and major repairs were done to the basin of the fountain in 2010. The St. James Court Art Show has taken place every year in October for nearly sixty years and has raised funds for maintaining the court and the fountain. Since 1978 the organizers have also funded a growing number of college scholarships for high school students.[84] How pleased my grandmother would be if she could witness the art show! I can only think that if she is an angel, as she imagined, she is flying over to enjoy the efforts of neighbors and visiting artists!

Unauthorized parking in St. James Court posed another danger. The fire department warned that they would not be able to pass by the cars if a fire broke out. Virginia earned attention in the Louisville newspaper for her efforts to curb illegal parking. The articles (undated) note that Virginia had just signed warrants for seven motorists to be taken to municipal court and that she had sworn to fourteen warrants the previous September. Punishments included a five-dollar fine and a charge of breach of peace.[85] When official channels failed, my grandmother crept out in the dark of night and let out the air from the tires of violators. She then found another means to slow down drivers and keep them off the grass. In a May 1952 letter, she told my mother that she was "building a stone wall at the Belgravia oval to keep the devils from driving across the grass." Belgravia Court is a lovely "walking court," not a street open to traffic, situated perpendicular to the south end of St. James Court. Currently it has various decorative barriers that impede the entrance of cars.

"Preaching on Monday and fighting in the alley on Tuesday"

Virginia also contributed to her church and to women's groups in Louisville. She addressed the Little Study Club (founded in 1925), a group of Louisville women who scheduled regular programs for their enrichment. At Calvary Episcopal Church in Louisville, my grandmother spoke to the Women's Auxiliary from around 1948 to 1954. She also taught an adult Sunday school class there, designed to prepare her listeners for the rector's sermon. However, her talks ranged beyond the scope of the rector's preaching. Moreover, they sometimes went overtime and outshone the sermon.

My grandmother remarked that her mother "wanted a son who would grow up to be a preacher. What she got was a girl who grew up preaching" (*Close Your Eyes*, 60). Her other audiences at Calvary included the Good Friday service, where she preached on "Forgiveness and Salvation through the Crucified Lord."[86] Furthermore, she preached at the Goodwill Chapel in Louisville and was invited to be the Episcopal representative at the chapel for Lent, including Ash Wednesday and Good Friday. She explained to my mother, "These people at the chapel are a forlorn folk who must at times feel that God has forgotten them. Our work is simple: to bring spiritual encouragement and assurance to them." My grandmother's preaching was so well received that the chapel invited her to deliver more sermons, and she gladly agreed. As she told it, the chapel representative said to her, "The la-di-da words of some of the robed preachers do not go over down here. These are simple and plain people who want a simple truth."[87]

Virginia's teaching and preaching had begun back in Cloverport during the summer of 1922. She taught Sunday school at the Methodist church, where her audience included Baptists, Methodists, Presbyterians, and two Jews, whose insights on the Hebrew scriptures she treasured. To prepare her classes, Virginia borrowed books from the Roman Catholic priest in town, but none of his congregants participated in her group. At the end of the classes, she invited all the class and most of the town, it seems, to a barbecue at her father's house. *Close Your Eyes* recounts some barbecue events and entertainment (*Close Your Eyes,* 12–20). The class members were joined by the undertaker; the Baptist, Methodist, Presbyterian, and Holy Roller ministers; and a "rabid" spiritualist known as "Wicked Wick" ("Devilish Dan" in *Close Your Eyes*). Wicked Wick was always accompanied by an invisible Indian maiden who conveyed supernatural insight as well as by a supposed female relative who traveled on his riverboat, the *White Dove,* and read a crystal ball, palms, and other media. All these folks came together for food, singing, and dancing. Virginia brought out the best in all of them and created bonds of community.

Preaching to the forlorn in a city entailed some risks. Virginia told in one letter that the Tuesday after her preaching at the chapel, a man came up to her in the alley behind the church and tried to steal her pocketbook. She swung her heavy purse and hit him in the jaw, but he got away. She had intended to sit on him and yell until help came! "Preaching on Monday, and fighting in the alley on Tuesday," she concluded. This was not my grandmother's only encounter with a thief. She was ready to take on whatever life brought her way.

My grandmother's height seems to have bolstered her strong spirit. Certainly she showed quick thinking in dangerous situations. One night around nine o'clock she was driving home in the pouring rain and stopped at a red light at Sixth and Oak Streets in Louisville. Sallie, her long-time household worker, had taken sick that morning. My grandmother had put her to bed for the day and had just taken her home. On the return trip, Virginia had forgotten to lock her car doors, and at the red light, a drunk man got in the front seat with her. No one was on the street because of the heavy rain. The man refused to get out and said he had no place to go. My grandmother quickly thought, "Jail, good old jail!" But how could she "keep him from popping" her? She decided to keep him interested but wondered, "What would interest him?" She thought, "Himself of course." The situation grew more frightening as she drove the five or so blocks between Oak and Magnolia Streets:

> So from Oak to Magnolia, I told him I knew just the place for him, room for himself, free eats, something going on all the time, and he would never forget his stay. By that time I turned Sixth at Magnolia on two wheels. Four MPs were standing under the police station shed. That did it! My unwelcome passenger called me every name in the book, and I drove down under the viaduct, drew up to the curb, and more perspiration streamed off me than I would ever shed in a Turkish Bath.[88]

The letter recounting this story has no date. Why were MPs standing at the police station? The Kentucky National Guard has assisted in keeping order during emergencies in Louisville around the time of the Kentucky Derby, the first Saturday in May, since 1936. The incident may have occurred around Derby time, when the MPs were regularly there.[89]

In another incident in December 1946 she entered the Piggly Wiggly around noon. As she recounted, "a holdup man came in and hid in the back. Jumped at me from a little door back of the refrigerator and told me to, 'Keep my mouth shut, it is a holdup.' ... I hollered as loud as I could, 'Why you little gun-toting shrimp, you'll not get my pocketbook.' The grocery boys chased him over fences through yards and in the alley, and the cops got him."[90] My grandmother foiled another thief who wanted her purse on a separate occasion. As she told the story, "Last night at a stop sign, a guy stepped up to the car and demanded my purse. [He wanted] me to give him my only dollars. Like hell I would! I told him I had a gun on the seat, and my finger on the trigger, and if he didn't get going, I would blow his belly open. He got away. So did I. I never carried a gun in my life."[91]

Still another robber got away from my grandmother despite her efforts. As she reported to my mother, "I went to the mail box around 11:00 p.m. and some smart guy grabbed my purse. It had two handles. He pulled one off. I popped him with my flash light and he got away. If I had had my cane, I could have hooked the handle around his ankle, tripped him up and sat on him until somebody came."[92] My mother telephoned when she received the letter about this robbery. A telephone call was costly in those days and saved for emergencies and extraordinary news. Worried that her mother would be in emotional distress, my mother instead found her still fuming that the thief had gotten away.

Why did my grandmother take such risks? Perhaps the everyday gambles of horse racing and the many characters she dealt with at racetracks emboldened her attitude toward crooks of all types. She displayed a keen sense of when the odds were in her favor and when they were against her. My grandmother's upbringing as the daughter of a prominent railroad president instilled in her a strong sense of responsibility for the neighborhood where she lived. She took seriously her role as president of the Saint James Court Association and interpreted her responsibilities broadly. Virginia's father used his social prominence generously, and Virginia followed his example. In a situation where something needed to be done, she would step forward to do it.

Across the Miles

Virginia traveled from Kentucky to Maryland every year to see us, her daughter and her daughter's family. She usually made the journey in July, after she went to Johns Hopkins for kidney stone treatments. We went to Kentucky as often as we could but always for Christmas and the Derby. My grandmother wrote about taking me to see Santa Claus when I was four (1951). I did not like him and remarked, "I don't trust anybody whose whiskers are tied on" (*Close Your Eyes*, 65). In a photo with Santa, my face shows skepticism if not distrust. Between visits my grandmother's letters helped keep the memories alive from the previous visit and prepared us for the excitement of the coming visit. One letter readied me for the goldfish she had gotten for me. "Tell Beverly the gold fish are named Swimmy, Finnie, and Minnie."[93] A few letters gave us updates on Donald, the duck that she'd adopted during one of our visits to St. James Court, and on my grand-

Beverly Mayne and Santa, 1951

father's impatience with him. To my mother she noted, "Tell Beverly that the duck is growing. I make your father take him to walk in the yard, and he, your father, curses and swears every step. It is a blessing that the duck is a duck and not a parrot."[94] My grandmother kept me posted on Donald's daily activities:

> I thought you would like to know how your duck is getting along. Every morning he swims in the dish pan, then he sits in his rocking chair and rocks while I fix his breakfast. When he eats and when I put his box in the sun, he puts his head under his wings and goes to sleep. Then I tip around so that I won't wake him up.[95]

In the fall of 1953, I entered first grade. My mother's notes tell about that school year:

> When Beverly entered the school house door I wanted for her what I had not known—an uninterrupted school year. So I stayed put. But I called home a great deal, and Virginia called her daughter. Mother's plea to come home early for Christmas was answered. She wrote, "Why don't you come home a week earlier at Christmas. That last week of school doesn't amount to a hoot." This was the Christmas of 1953—Virginia's last.
>
> You, of course, realize I did not know this. She called several times asking me to please come early. You know what I did? You are right. I took Beverly out of school much to the horror of much more experienced mothers and I left early this Christmas of 1953, getting on the day coach for the all night trip which did not end until well into the next day, with a six year old, Christmas presents, Santa Claus. Even to this day I wonder what ever possessed me to try that collapsible doll buggy. Usually Christmas toys just remain collapsed, but this doll buggy would suddenly start to rise, and I would leap up and smack it flat again, hoping that Beverly would not discover that Santa Claus rode the B & O that early in December. Then the change of trains, endless suitcases, shopping bags, leggings, gloves, you name it, and I was either coming or going with same.

Before my first school year ended, my grandmother was gone. She gave a talk to the ladies of Calvary Episcopal Church in Louisville on Tuesday, April 6, 1954. On Thursday, April 8, she died of a heart attack during a telephone conversation with a friend. The news spread through the church on Palm Sunday, and the funeral took place on Monday, April 12, at a funeral home. Why there and not Calvary, I am not sure. Mourners from the Goodwill Chapel and the Salvation Army joined the Calvary parishioners, as did the many friends and family members of Virginia's household workers. They reassured each other and my mother that "Miss Virginia was ready" and that God "needed her to help get heaven ready for Easter." Surely, they said, "This was going to be the biggest Easter Glory ever seen, because Miss Virginia could fix things up."[96] My mother left the story of my grandmother's funeral unfinished. Notes in pencil add the St. James Court neighbors and some policemen to the groups of attendees. The text of my mother's narrative, "Ah, Dear Readers," records this:

> On the eighth day of April, of the year 1954, I planned to meet my husband in town to pick out the long dreamed of rug for my living room. I was going to surprise Mother with the news when she came. My bare floor worried Virginia. We walked the Olsen display room and I hurried on home after that to be there for Beverly's first grade to let out. On my door step sat a beautiful box of pansies. I hurried to the back border willow tree outside the dining room to put these lovely plants in the ground. The ring of the phone sounded. Why not just let it ring? No, I would put the trowel down, run around to the side as its rings sounded in my ears. This was the phone call to tell me of my mother's sudden death. Virginia was gone. She was 59. On May 28th, 1954 she would have had her 60th birthday. We left for Kentucky that evening. On Holy Monday we left her in a small cemetery on a Kentucky hillside.

My grandmother had written to my mother,

> When you reach fifty, I will be gone, but there will inevitably follow for you a fifteen-year period of

adjustment, a time to alter your established mode of living and to so arrange your affairs as to procure for yourself sufficient security before you are sixty-five, when wise men say one is old. After that all you need or desire will be a little comfort and, God willing, a little kindness.

Sadly my mother was not yet thirty-eight when my grandmother died. Fifteen years later, my mother had published the four books of her mother's writings, appeared on the *Today Show* in New York, traveled the eastern half of the United States for book signings, and escaped the pressures of fame and financial conflicts to take a voyage in the Mediterranean to the Holy Land, a trip that she had dreamed years before of taking with her mother.

Virginia Cleveland Mayne in Old Jerusalem, March 1963

My mother climbed the streets of Old Jerusalem that she and her mother had dreamed of walking, and her tears flowed amid the exhilaration. Similarly when my husband, daughter, and I visited Venice for the first time in 1990, tears joined me to my mother's spirit and her "hillbilly hop" of joy at the sight of and memory of her favorite city's beauty. As the orchestras played in turn around St. Mark's Square, I perceived fully the delight she'd experienced at the unparalleled sights, sounds, and tastes of the city called La Serenissima.

Virginia Cleveland Mayne in her home office, 1965

Chapter 2

"Glory Three Times Also and Amen Twice": The Path to Publication and Success

⁂

The keys on the 1908 typewriter clacked as my mother pounded out multiple onionskin copies of my grandmother's writings, working from the copies that were typed and handwritten in May 1952, before the fire. The typewriter's age seemed to bond her to the world of her mother's youth. The pictures she arranged around her workspace bridged one generation to the next. In the photo taken after the publication of *O Ye Jigs & Juleps!* and *Credos & Quips*, my mother looks out over the old typewriter. Folders, pens, and pencils sit neatly on a usually cluttered working space, a table that my father first built for a dining room and then reinforced to serve as a desk. The two published books stand before the typewriter and testify to the fulfillment of work, love, and prayer. Virginia Cary Hudson Cleveland embraces her six-month-old child (my mother) in a photo on the wall, reproduced on p. xii and several other pictures of my grandmother encircle my mother seated at the table. Mother smiles softly, not fully, pushing her eyebrows slightly upward to accentuate eyes that reveal both the determined intensity of her achievement and the sadness at the story behind the two books and the passage through life that the photographs indicate.

Once she had assembled a manuscript and organized her onionskin carbon copies, we walked the mile and a half from our house to the Landover Hills post office and mailed the manuscript off to publishers. A self-taught editor, my mother had a solid literary education but no experience in the professional book world. She received advice on manuscript preparation wherever she could get it, mostly from friends and how-to manuals. She approached publishers directly after locating addresses and guidelines for submitting manuscripts. She contacted one agency, but she knew no literary agents until she had one! She made no changes to my grandmother's texts. Seventeen times we heard the noise of rejection; either the thud of the returned manuscript hitting the floor, or the doorbell ringing when Bill, the letter carrier, could not bear to let it drop. "Mrs. Mayne," he would say, "I'm sorry, but it's back again." Producing manuscripts, facing rejection, and trying again constituted the fabric of daily living.

Several years later, my mother assembled a scrapbook about the story of *O Ye Jigs & Juleps!* She kept all the rejection letters as well as the testimonies to success. The negative responses came from a range of publishers, both books and magazines. Several letters record negotiations with a so-called vanity press, which would not budge from a price over $1,000. Some rejections provided an explanation. Others were form letters with not even an indication of the date:

> We regret that we are unable to use the enclosed material. Thank you for giving us the opportunity to consider it. The editors.

> Thank you for submitting this material. After careful consideration, we regret that it doesn't suit our present needs. Please excuse this impersonal reply but it's impossible to send an individual letter to each contributor, much as we'd like to. Please try us again. The editors.

The dated letters fall between 1958 and 1959. The senders include the Abington Press, Curtis Brown (agent), *Coronet* (magazine), Thomas Y. Crowell Co., Doubleday & Co., *Good Housekeeping*, Grosset and Dunlap, Harcourt Brace & Co., Harper & Row, *Harper's Magazine*, the *New Yorker, Reader's Digest*, Simon & Schuster Inc. An additional note in my mother's writing records other refusals by *Esquire, Ladies Home Journal,* and *McCall's.*

A *Saturday Review* article by John G. Fuller (1913–1990) demonstrates humor and empathy for my mother as he fired back at the publishing houses that rejected her manuscript. In the mid-1960s, Fuller was promoting his books about extraterrestrial encounters, *Incident at Exeter* and *The Interrupted Journey* (1966), at book signings around the country. He and my mother met at one such event, if not more. She must have shared her rejection letters with him. Fuller, author of several nonfiction books and many articles and a writer for the *Saturday Review*, wrote sympathetically and in detail about the rejections my mother had endured:

> [The manuscript for *O Ye Jigs & Juleps!*] also had accumulated a massive train of the mellifluous prose that characterizes the rejection slips that every writer worth his salt has amassed *ad nauseam.* The marvel of it all was the varied and gentle euphemisms employed to convey exactly the same sentiment: your manuscript is NG. Thanks, anyway, try someone else. The Thomas Y. Crowell Company, for instance, sent the manuscript merrily back with: "We are sorry that it does not seem to us to suggest a suitable addition to our small general list, and we are therefore returning it ..." Harcourt, Brace & World propelled the manuscript back home with: "We want you to know your manuscript has received careful reading by one or more of our editors, and we do sincerely regret that it does not fit our publication plans ... Please accept our thanks for thinking of us, and

our best wishes for success ..." Doubleday offered these sentiments: "We have carefully considered the manuscript which you kindly submitted to us, and regret that we are unable to undertake its publication ... Our decision in regard to your book reflects merely our own editorial need and our own judgment of its sales possibilities on our particular list ..." Grosset & Dunlap offered these condolences: "We appreciate your letting us see your manuscript, but we are sorry to report that we would not be able to consider it for publication as it is not appropriate to our list ... We wish you success in finding the right publisher ..." Simon & Schuster said: "We do appreciate your having let us see the manuscript, and regret that it is not something we can use ..." Curtis Brown, Ltd., the literary agents, wrote: "I am sorry to say that I don't think we can help you. The material you mention does not appear to be anything we could be hopeful of placing. Thank you for thinking of us ..." *Harper's* magazine commented: "We regret to say, after careful consideration, that we cannot use the manuscript which you have sent us. Thank you for giving us a chance to consider it." Wrote the *New Yorker*: "We regret that we are unable to use the enclosed material. Thank you for giving us the opportunity to consider it." There were others. Almost as many as there were magazines and publishing houses, each with the same well-tuned phrase, so softly written and so hard to take.

Fuller closed with seeming delight by remarking that "a new collection by the same author has appeared in the bookstalls, and it failed to collect a single rejection slip. The title: *Flapdoodle, Trust & Obey.* Ironically enough, though, it is published by one of the houses that had previously joined the rejection parade of *O Ye Jigs & Juleps!*, Harper & Row."[97]

My mother's notes for "Ah, Dear Readers" recount the experience of rejection in heavy, heartfelt words. They also explain her first efforts at publishing when she lacked experience with the process. My readers may not know or remember that photocopying in the 1950s was not easy. My mother had to walk about a mile to the bus stop, then take a thirty-minute bus ride into Washington, DC, and then walk to a place that produced photocopies on thick, smelly, heavy sheets of paper. She took the 9:03 Greyhound bus into the city, hoping to wait for the copies that same day, but often she had to make a second trip to retrieve the originals and the copies and mail them to a publisher. The costs mounted up for multiple mailings.

> It was very hard, it still is. I was ever so slow. In 1958 I took the essays out and made up my mind that I definitely was going to try very hard to have them published. What does one do, and how does one start to have something published? You see, I was right back where my mother had been [not knowing where to start the process]. A copy of Good Housekeeping was sitting on my table; I picked it up and read that a Mr. Berlin was the President. So—I thought I will just send the essays to him; registered, air-mail—special delivery. This I did! Three to four months later a Mr. Herbert Mayes wrote me saying they had enjoyed the essays, but they could not use them. They were not magazine material—however, to send him additional ones. He would see what he could do. I couldn't send him additional ones—I didn't have any more. You can see how impossible this was. Then I started, I mailed the manuscript as if there were no tomorrow from 1958 to 1960. I do not drive. My shoes are my wheels, and the walk to the post office from my former residence was a good three-fourths of a mile. I walked in the summer's sun and in the winter's cold; usually Beverly was with me.

Many a time we barely made the required postage. After a while the post office employees would remark when they saw us coming, "Well, maybe this time." I went to New York, but no one would see me. I didn't have an appointment. An appointment with whom? I didn't know anyone. I tried the Vanity presses, but their requested funds in order to publish material stopped me. No monthly payments would they hear of. The bank would not let me have the necessary funds. Give up, I would not.

As I think back, it was at this point I reminded myself of G. R. R. Rosenthal's Sins of the Saints. In the chapter "Neglect of Prayer," he says this, "Much of our disappointment with the results of prayer is due to what one of the most beautiful of our collects calls 'The ignorance of our asking.'"

At last, a connection through Episcopal church channels brought the essays to the attention of Martha Johnson and Doris Thompson, literary agents and co-owners of a bookstore in Washington, DC. My mother writes about this unforeseen happening. It seemed magical, even miraculous, to her.

I had copies for my friends to enjoy. Fanny Morrell typed many for me. A set of these copies reached Madge (Mrs. Howard) Arnold. Her husband is the Rev. Howard Arnold, the brother of my former rector, Kenneth Arnold. Madge truly loved the essays. On the second day of January in 1961 my telephone rang. The voice at the other end of the line informed me that she was Martha Johnson at the Francis Scott Key Bookshop. She and Mrs. Doris Thompson were literary agents. They had the essays and planned to try and work with them, and the Bishop's wife, Mrs. Angus Dun, had brought the essays to her. Well, for heavens' sake, isn't this wonderful! I thought, but how did the Bishop's wife get them? The Bishop and Mrs. Dun had been invited down to the Arnold's for dinner. Madge had gotten the essays out after dinner to read. She told Mrs. Dun of my many efforts to have them published. Indeed, the "Angel of the Lord encampth around and about,"[98] and the Good Lord had known exactly where to send them. How thrilled I was to have somebody to help me at long last, and such wonderful people. So the little essays had a fairy godmother. She handed them to the ones holding the magic wand. I could tell they loved the little pieces; this was the nicest part.

A biography had to be written, you can well imagine what that meant, with the accent on the first ten to eleven years of my mother's life. I am the eldest of three—my mother was an only child. There wasn't the usual Auntie or Uncle to fill in the years. My father is eight years older than my mother. When she was ten, he was eighteen. I wrote cousins. Then we had no originals. Would my affidavit be acceptable? Mrs. Johnson sent the essays to Harper and Row. We went into deep sadness when they turned us down.

One morning Mrs. Johnson called to say a young man from the Macmillan Company had read the essays. He was delighted with them. This young man, James Gregg, intended to try and invest his own funds, should Macmillan turn us down. February passed, and we waited and we wondered. March passed and we wondered and we waited. April offered the same, no change. On the eleventh day of May 1961, the essays officially became the property of the Macmillan Company under the working title of "An Afternoon's Stroll." They would be published! I was hilarious! My job was done! Now I could put

73

away the endless papers, letters and the like which had filled my dining room for so many years. In October 1961, I moved. My expenses doubled. During this period I did baby-sitting in this new neighborhood to help pay expenses.

On the first day of December 1961, Macmillan gave us a title—*Jigs & Juleps!*; the bookshop added *O Ye* right from the Episcopal Prayer Book. Some five hundred hand written announcements of the publication were mailed upon the heels of Christmas cards, then Easter came early this year of 1962. A small formal appearing card arrived telling me that the official publication date was April 16, 1962, Holy Monday. It was on Holy Monday of 1954 that I left my mother on that Kentucky hillside. The Good Lord had worked it out even unto the letter of the day; this memorial I wanted.

I was delighted with the finished product; the editor Betty Bartelme had indeed done a beautiful job.[99] The artist Karla Kuskin I have never met. How I would love to see her. The Francis Scott Key Bookshop had a debut party for O Ye Jigs & Juleps! I met those from New York who had shared this interest for so many months.

The Episcopal Book Club, Hillspeak, Eureka Springs, Arkansas announced their summer selection. It was you know what—Yes—This would have delighted and thrilled my mother more than anything else. How she loved her church.

Two weeks after publication, one of my great-grandfather's relatives who had been helping my mother's research by searching for family records and photographs finally found a treasure in a trunk that had belonged to my great-grandfather's sister. The now well-known portrait of Virginia Cary Hudson at age ten had been tucked in the trunk after my great-grandfather had sent it to his sister. Thus, another woman who preserved memories contributed to restoring Virginia's identity. The photo surfaced too late to appear on the book jacket of *O Ye Jigs & Juleps!*, but it arrived in the nick of time for my mother to display at book appearances and prove that a ten-year-old Virginia Cary Hudson did in fact exist.

My mother's account moves to its close as she explains another significant date in her history of publishing *O Ye Jigs & Juleps!*

> On May 27, 1962, the little book made its debut on the best seller list of the New York Times. You know what the following day, May the 28th happened to be? My mother's birthday!
>
> Still Virginia's daughter said nothing about all the rejection slips she had at home. She did not tell her story until the little book was number three on the New York Times list. Then I couldn't stand it any longer. I got out these slips, and I told my story and this is it. Every time a manuscript comes thru the mail for me to read, I smile. I am the last person in the world to have sent to me anything to be published. One who tried so long and so hard, and got absolutely no place until I was adopted by Johnson & Thompson.
>
> I have told you of the joy, of the hard work, of the prayers and best wishes of so many. All of these accompany anything of great worth. Let me add there has also been some sorrow. Every time I see the little book, my heart leaps up, yet every time I ask myself: "Why, oh why couldn't she have lived to witness all this?"
>
> Let me close by telling you, if any of you have something you want to do very badly, I hope this homespun little story will give you a spark of the spirit of "never say die." Say your prayers and keep trying.

May 27, 1962, had been set as the original publication date for *O Ye Jigs & Juleps!*, but the date was advanced to April 16. The prepublication reviews began to appear in February 1962. It was the beginning of what turned out to be a debate over the authenticity of the essays. My mother never expected that writings so dear to her would be contested to such a degree that some doubted the existence of her beloved mother and challenged whether there was ever a fire at 1453 St. James Court. I still feel intensely the anguish of my mother's shock at the painful confrontations. As she told me and wrote in the notes I have, someone from *Time* magazine, bent on exposing the book's authorship by Virginia Cary Hudson as a fraud, derided my mother, claiming that the 1952 destruction of the attic at 1453 St. James Court was a "convenient fire."

My years of studying women's writings as a scholar provide a historical perspective on the *Time* writer's contempt. Such a long-range view does not diminish the insult but situates it within the centuries-old disparagement of female achievement. Some said that the great medieval visionary and interpreter of the Bible, Hildegard of Bingen (1098–1179), could not have written the works that she clearly authored or composed her music or designed illustrations, and on it goes.[100] Many other women authors had their very identity questioned and their works presumed to be forgeries. The criteria for evaluation of authenticity have not always been applied with adequate knowledge and fairness. Virginia's writings were scrutinized in some cases without thorough investigation of her historical identity, and they suffered a fate not unlike that of works composed by women in other centuries.

Reviews of *O Ye Jigs & Juleps!*

Reconstructing the history of how readers reacted to *O Ye Jigs & Juleps!* is possible because my mother compiled a large *Jigs & Juleps!* scrapbook. She included not only reviews, which she eventually purchased through a service, but also personal written testimonies, letters to editors, focus articles, and other memorabilia. The very first review in February 1962 raised no doubts about the essays, reading simply:

> A frank and funny diary of a church-going Episcopalian, but not overly pious ten-year-old girl in a small town at the turn of the century. A cheerful little book, about her friends, of all ages, her mischief-making, and her insight into the grown-ups' lives. With gay, tidy drawings by Karla Kuskin.[101]

A month later (March 29, 1962), the *Woodford County Sun*, the local paper for Versailles, Kentucky, where so much family history had taken place, featured a story about the new book entitled "Happy Landings." The author reported that my grandfather, still living in Louisville and visiting friends in Versailles, had come with *O Ye Jigs & Juleps!*:

> Mr. Kirtley Cleveland had dropped by the *Sun* and left us with a book written by Virginia Cary Hudson. Apparently this little book was written when the author was ten years old, or about 1904, and was set in Versailles. Its title is "O Ye Jigs & Juleps!" and it is hilarious.

The article writer included excerpts from Virginia's essays "Everlasting Life," "Spring," "The Library," and "China and Religion" and then added another especially vivid statement from the little book: "If I have to go to Hell, I sure hope I go to the one for Episcopalians, and don't by mistake, get pushed in that horn punching, and tail wagging, red hot blazing one." The writer concluded the piece with the complimentary opinion that "this is a child's collection of impressions, it is an adult hilarious come-uppance. It is a spicy slice of small-town Americana in the early 1900's. As the author herself would say. ' ... Hallelujah! Glory three times also, and Amen twice.'"

The *L. and N. Magazine* proudly featured a review in October 1962, noting that the author's daughter Ann was working for the railroad in Louisville and that the author's father had worked with the L. & N. and "closely associated" railroads. The reviewer postulated that R. N. Hudson was responsible for preserving the essays. "Mr. Hudson, a cultured gentleman, was quick to recognize literary ability when he saw it." In addition, the reviewer answered critics who doubted that "a junior miss could be so perceptive." He affirmed that "friends, who knew the author, both as a child and as a grown woman, have no doubt at all. They say the book 'sounds just like her!'"[102]

Hometown pride in Virginia's authorship was followed by a debate between doubters and believers in Atlanta. A letter to the editors expressed the doubt that the letters were written by a ten-year-old. My mother and grandmother had met with a credibility gap. Yet defenders arose as well. A series of letters in the *Atlanta Journal* published opinions from both sides (April 4, 9, and 11, 1962). Selections below from the letters demonstrate that the authenticity of my grandmother's authorship provoked a lively dispute.

One letter sharply denounced the claim that my grandmother wrote the essays at age ten.

No Time for "Jigs" Says Author Hyman

> The Editors: I have to agree with the gentleman who wrote to you doubting the authenticity of the book "O Ye Jigs & Juleps!" I admit I don't grasp his Biblical analogy, but taking into consideration the style, the point-of-view, subject matter, slick clichés, and what-not, I can't accept for a minute that this was written by a 10-year-old child …
> MAC HYMAN. Cordele.

The *Atlanta Journal*'s editor(s) replied, "Sorry, but the evidence shows that Jigs & Juleps! really did come from the pen of Virginia Cary Hudson."

An opposing view exuded delight at reading the essays and pined for the days when children expressed such clear and exquisite thoughts.

"Jigs" Warmed Reader's Heart

The Editors: "O Ye Jigs & Juleps!" was another of the best things that has happened to the *Journal* and its readers.

I was 10 years old when I first played the organ at the Baptist Church in Acworth. The first song I played was "There Is a Fountain Filled With Blood." Since the little girl mentioned this song in her journal I'd like to think she was present that memorable morning.

With her inherent talent for telling the plain, unvarnished truth about everything and everybody, she might have written this one small sentence about the little girl at the organ: "She was scared."

I'm rather glad to have been taken in by "Jigs & Juleps!," enfolded in the sheer delightfulness of a child's unfolding mind.

I was so intoxicated with joy that should there be any weeds in this wonderful garden where words are strung together in lovely magic abandon portraying the infinite reaches of a child's crystal-clear mind, I am unable to see weeds, being blinded by exquisite beauty.

You might well say I am charm-bound in a child's Garden of Enchantment where no weeds grow and no discordant doubts mar a pleasing euphony. Oh, how wonderful to be so naive!

A friend points out that she doubts any of today's children could have written this book. She says their minds are too cluttered with too many things, and I think that's the truth.

LORA STOKELY. Atlanta.

Ms. Stokely demonstrated a certain flair for language herself in her recounting of the heights of her delight at the essays, describing their world as an enchanted garden where weeds do not grow and harmony resounds. Such imagery of the sights and sounds of gardens recalls many gardens in literature and reflects the pen of a talented person, who, as she revealed, played the organ at ten.

Another writer, whose letter was published on April 4, defended the essays with the memory her mother reported of schooling in the early twentieth century and with a knowledge of literary history, namely of the Brontë sisters, celebrated poets and novelists of the nineteenth century.

Easy to Believe "Jigs" Authentic

The Editors: Re: "O Ye Jigs & Juleps!"
...
I don't find it at all hard to believe that these essays were written by a 10-year-old girl. My mother was 10 at the time of this young lady and assures me that in those days English composition was stressed in schools as science is today. It was not at all unusual for a 10-year-old in those days to be able to read, write and spell. The Brontes were quite young when they began to write, at a much earlier period.

I think that the series is as delightful and refreshing as a drink at a clear mountain stream. I certainly do not feel it is an assault on the Bible, and I think it quite possible the child was horrified at the hymns sung by the other church when she was familiar with the songs in her hymnal.

Let's hope that your other readers will accept the series for its humor and not try to make issues where none exist.

Mrs. R. L. Gordon. Atlanta.

"Delightful as a drink at a clear mountain stream"—clearly Virginia inspired some of her readers to employ poetic language themselves to capture her gifts. Both Mrs. Gordon and Ms. Stokely connected with Virginia's emotive reaction to the language of "There Is a Fountain Filled with Blood." As a child, Ms. Stokely was afraid, apparently, at the hymn's words and not at the experience of playing the organ in church, and Mrs. Gordon allows the possibility that young Virginia was "horrified" by the hymns of "the other church." Ms. Stokely and Mrs. Gordon's comments shed some light on listeners' reactions to styles of church hymnody. They also show that female readers were generally more receptive to Virginia's authorship than male readers.

In a letter published April 9, 1962, an eight-year-old boy was the next to voice his defense of Virginia's essays and to criticize the view of the incredulous letter above, which had been penned by his own father. A house was divided by *O Ye Jigs & Juleps!*

More About "Juleps" From Hyman House

The Editors: Concerning that skeptical letter written by my father, Mac Hyman, and published the other day in your paper relating to the literary authenticity of "O Ye Jigs & Juleps!," I would like to say on behalf of myself and my sisters that we are not in accord with our father in this matter, particularly now that you have revealed publicly that the aforementioned book was written by its author, Virginia Cary Hudson.

...

As for myself, I still feel that this book is brilliantly conceived and masterfully handled. I find in it a remarkable use of impressionistic vernacular, a harmonious and subtle use of sentence pacing, and an extremely skillful management of verisimilitude. TOM HYMAN, Age 8. Cordele.

The *Atlanta Journal's* editors replied, "Kids are getting smarter all the time." One may wonder if any readers of the *Atlanta Journal* commented on this letter, namely on the vocabulary, which takes on a quite learned flavor in the last two sentences.

A fifth grader, well acquainted with the prose of ten-year-olds, arose to second Tom Hyman's defense of Virginia's authorship. Penny Gail Pennington claimed to write for her father and asserted that Patrick Watters, age nine, wrote some of the columns that appeared in the paper.

Sergeants, Jigs, and 10-Year-Olds

The Editors: I am constrained to accept the views of Tom Hyman and suggest that his father is wrong in doggedly insisting on the possibility, yea, the probability, that it was not Virginia Cary Hudson who wrote "O Ye Jigs & Juleps!"

My father (Mr. John Pennington) likewise had his doubts about the matter, until he read Tom's letter in the paper. Then he went to the bookshelf and took down his tattered copy of "No Time for Sergeants," supposedly by Mr. Mac Hyman, thumbing rapidly back and forth and mumbling to himself something to the effect that maybe it was one of Mr. Hyman's formerly 10-year-old daughters that wrote the book. Or maybe Tom.

Your incisive verbal coup de grace in answer to Mr. Hyman's doubting letter was most impressive. Worth quoting. "Sorry," you said, "but the evidence shows that Jigs & Juleps! really did come from the pen of Virginia Cary Hudson." A telling blow, after which there really was no need to cite the evidence. The kind of forthright editorial page journalism I quote occasionally in the fifth-grade classroom at Smyrna Elementary School.

And besides, why should I doubt the abilities of a 10-year-old of another generation? I write most of my father's better pieces, and I happen to know that

Patrick Watters, age 9, is responsible for some of the better columns that appear on this page.

PENNY GAIL PENNINGTON, Age 10. Smyrna.

By April 1962, *O Ye Jigs & Juleps!* had captured attention from the national news media. *Life* magazine included it with four other books in its "Life Guide," calling *O Ye Jigs & Juleps!* a "tiny and hilarious collection of precocious essays" and including a small drawing of Virginia at a typewriter with the caption, "In 1904 a precocious pixie of 10 wrote sprightly essays just now published."[103]

Just a few days later, in the April 30, 1962, issue, *Newsweek* published a review entitled "Sleepers Awake." There are some inaccuracies in the review. My mother did not "rescue" the essays from the attic after my grandmother's death but found them with her about two years before she died. Moreover, the reviewer, while praising the esteem Martha and Doris held in the Washington literary world, overstates their role in publishing the book. Still the review informs us about the stature and past discoveries of Johnson and Thompson.

> In the tiny, two-story building which houses the Francis Scott Key Bookshop, the pervading aroma of book dust mixes with the scent of home-baked bread. With equal felicity, the shop—bought 23 years ago by a pair of widows in the Washington, D.C., section of Georgetown—manages to blend a homey atmosphere with an imposing Capital clientele. The browsers may include Dean Acheson, Walter Lippmann, or any one of a score of diplomats and senators—and coffee is sometimes served.
>
> For all their air of running a gift shoppe, Doris Thompson, 55, and Martha Johnson, 58, are among the nation's shrewdest hands at spotting a likely literary property. They discovered "Carp's Washington"—a successful book of two years ago made up of forgotten writing by a nineteenth-century newsman—and

they were among the earliest boosters of a then unpublished novel called "To Kill a Mockingbird." This spring, the Mesdames Thompson and Johnson are largely responsible for the publication of what promises to be the sleeper bestseller of the season. This is a small book of essays called "O Ye Jigs & Juleps!," the work of a 10 year-old Southern girl who wrote it in 1904.

Though formally on sale for the first time last week, "O Ye Jigs & Juleps!" actually is in its third printing; the first two editions already have been gobbled up by bookstores around the nation. Some 1,500 copies have gone to customers of the Francis Scott Key, delighted by the author's brisk and arresting observation of life as it was lived in a sleepy Kentucky town 60 years ago.

It was a customer—and at that, the wife of the Episcopal Bishop of Washington, Mrs. Angus Dun—who brought "Jigs" to the shop's attention. After Virginia (she became Mrs. Kirtley Cleveland in 1914) died suddenly in 1954, her daughter rescued the essays from the attic. In 1960, she took them to the family pastor who turned them over to Mrs. Dun who passed them on to Martha Johnson. Assured by a Kentucky friend that the essays were no hoax, she changed the names "to protect people's privacy" but otherwise, she insists, "it's just as it was written."

"We haven't gotten rich," says Mrs. Thompson, "but it's been a successful, rewarding adventure. When you have a personal bookshop, you're in it for the psychic pay."

As the agents, Martha and Doris received 10 percent of the royalties.

The *Newsweek* review relays the book's success with excitement and describes with admiration and even affection the booksellers and the enterprise of owning a small neighborhood bookshop. When I was in Washington in the mid-1990s, I stopped in the shop and met a staff member; she had heard about the fame of her predecessors and the little book. Now sadly I've learned that the bookshop, like so many others, closed, perhaps due to the opening of the larger Barnes & Noble in Georgetown, which in turn closed in December 2011.[104]

At some point prior to the book's publication, the Francis Scott Key hosted a party. *Publishers Weekly* reported on it with news of the phenomenal sales before publication, describing the shop's window as "decorated … simply but enticingly with copies of the book and silver julep mugs with sprigs of mint sticking up."[105] A few imperfect old Polaroid pictures from the scrapbook show the celebration.

Left to right: Lewis Mayne, Betty Bartelme, James Gregg, Beverly Mayne, Virginia Mayne, Doris Thompson, and Martha Johnson with copies of O Ye Jigs & Juleps! *at the Francis Scott Key Bookshop, 1962*

Martha Johnson (left), co-owner of the Francis Scott Key Bookshop, with a julep cup and O Ye Jigs & Juleps!, *and Virginia Cleveland Mayne (right) holding the book and the photo of her mother and herself at six months old, 1962*

Mrs. Dun celebrated her role in the book's discovery, as recounted by Rose MacMurray in the April 8, 1962, article "Bishop's Wife Says of Book: Hallelujah, Glory, and Amen (Twice)" in the *Washington Post*. At that point, twenty-five thousand copies of the book had been ordered before publication. Based on the article, MacMurray seems to have known nothing about my mother's years of work or the first rejection of the manuscript when submitted by Johnson and Thompson.

> A chintz-covered scrapbook has made a literary talent scout out of Mrs. Angus Dun, wife of the Episcopal Bishop of Washington. It's a new turn to an old hobby for Mrs. Dun, who, after a long stretch as a bookworm, doesn't mind saying that she loves books as much as people. And she adds: "At my age, if you read constantly, you should be able to recognize a good one."
>
> Mrs. Dun's "recognizing" came about when a rector friend of the family turned up with a scrapbook one of his parishioners had found in an attic.
>
> "When he read the manuscript to Bishop Dun and myself, I knew it must be published," said Mrs. Dun. "So all I did was take it to my friend, Martha Johnson, at the Francis Scott Key bookshop. Mrs. Johnson showed the manuscript to Macmillan. And now (with a smiling quotation from her literary discovery) 'Hallelujah! Glory three times also, and Amen twice'—here is the book!" she said.
>
> Ms. MacMurray observes that, "Virginia's highly original thoughts combine religion, ethics, small town atmosphere and humor in a way that reminds some readers of the spirited young heroine of 'To Kill a Mockingbird.' The difference, of course, is that 'Scout' of Mockingbird fame was fictional, whereas Virginia was very real."

According to Mrs. Dun, Martha Johnson had taken pains to authenticate the characters in the essays:

Martha Johnson got in touch with a friend who still lived in the little southern town and verified the actual characters. "The names have been changed," Mrs. Dun explained, "so there would be no invasion of privacy—But, otherwise, every word is just as Virginia wrote it 60 years ago. She stuttered, you see, and hated stuttering—and an inspired teacher let her write down all the thoughts and ideas and observations she wanted so much to express."

To some degree, Mrs. Dun identified with the ten-year old Virginia:

"I grew up in a small town like Virginia's and I remember all the same things—the Bissell sweeper, the ice-cream freezer on the back porch, the cisterns cleaned every spring. It's so remarkable that her book has preserved a whole way of life—absolutely intact, like Pompeii."

"Perhaps I was more than just practical," she laughed, "because when I was 10, I remember my aunt telling my mother, 'You must understand that Kitty isn't bad; she's truly wicked!' So I sympathize with Virginia, I really do."

"And I'm very glad," concludes Mrs. Dun, with natural Episcopalian pride, "that she had the bishop."

Mrs. Dun herself composed an article for *Cathedral Age* (Spring 1962), the magazine of the Episcopal Diocese of Washington, DC. Under the title, "Finding a Book," she recounted the details of the evening when she and the bishop drove down to Leeland, Maryland (in southern Prince George's County), for dinner with the rector of St. Barnabas Church, Howard Arnold, and his wife, Madge. Howard read from the essays after dinner, and the group laughed "until the tears ran." They all agreed that the essays should be published. As Mrs. Dun told the details,

I borrowed the manuscript and a day or two later I walked with it to the Francis Scott Key Book Shop, wondering a little in the grey of a cold morning whether the themes were really as funny as they had seemed in the lamplight at Leeland. With some hesitation, I pushed myself, package in hand, towards Mrs. Johnson's desk. She looked the quintessence of before Christmas weariness.

Although Mrs. Johnson protested that she could not read the manuscript before Christmas, she nonetheless called Mrs. Dun, a friend and esteemed customer, at nine the next morning. "Her voice had taken on new life," according to Mrs. Dun. Mrs. Johnson, unable to put down the manuscript until she finished it, found the essays "delightful" and had already called a friend in Virginia's hometown to verify the authenticity of the characters. My mother would soon learn that she had enthusiastic agents who would become lifelong friends, and the book was published little more than a year later.

Following the very favorable review in the April *Newsweek*, *O Ye Jigs & Juleps!* won attention and praise from the *New York Times Book Review* on May 13, 1962, with Lewis Nichols's "In 1904 When She Was 10."

Back in 1904, a young lady of 10 put down some reflections on the state of the world for her boarding school teacher. Fortunately, like the world, these failed to perish (in the former case it perhaps wasn't through not trying) and now they have been put together under the title of "O Ye Jigs & Juleps!" by Virginia Cary Hudson. Delightful is the word for it, whoever you are, and if you can remember the decades roundabout 1904, you can add the word, haunting.

Virginia was a combination brat and acute observer of the human scene, more closely a sister to Penrod than to Holden Caulfield. She had definite thoughts about school and about Spring, about Church, China and the neighbors. If you're about Penrod's present age now, you'll remember those iron benches that stood in every garden the length of Main Street. Hear Virginia, and be carried back: "When we sit on her garden bench, I get to hurting. Those iron grapes sure are hard. Mrs. McLean is fatter in the back than I am and I guess that is why she can sit there so long." ...

Some of Virginia's thoughts sound as though Machiavelli had rewritten Emily Post—to the greater good and glory of all concerned. "Etiquette is what you are doing and saying when people are looking and listening," she remarks. "What you are thinking is your business. Thinking is not etiquette."

Virginia no longer is living now, and her book was assembled by her daughter, Virginia Cleveland Mayne. As a point of view in a troubled time, however, you can do far worse than accept the version of the *Benedicite* that she left behind: "O ye Sun and Moon, oh ye beans and roses, oh ye Jigs & juleps, Bless ye the Lord, Praise Him and Magnify Him Forever. Amen."

Mr. Nichols, who has his own memories, conducts the "In and Out of Books" column in the Book Review.

What could be said about the review but "Glory three times also and amen twice!"—one of my grandmother's favorite exclamations. The *New York Times*! Nothing says success and celebration like New York. "If you can make it there ..." A reviewer for the *New York Times* not only appreciated and praised Virginia Cary Hudson's special gift and the sparkling acuity of her words, but he also recommended reading the little book. Nichols was a well-respected reviewer and an astute predictor of success. During World War II, he had gained a "reputation as one of the most accurate prognosticators of the probable success of new Broadway plays and musicals." For a decade from 1957, he served as assistant book review editor for the *Times* and wrote the "In and Out of Books" column for the *Book Review*.[106]

Episcopalians manifested enthusiasm for the little book. The Episcopal Book Club chose *O Ye Jigs & Juleps!* as its summer selection. On May 14, 1962, H. L. Foland wrote my mother from Eureka Springs, Arkansas—home of the book club—with obvious excitement and the news that the book club was taking 9,250 copies, with an arrangement from Macmillan for them to have more if they should need them. The book club mailing of *O Ye Jigs & Juleps!* included a second book entitled *Scripture and the Faith. Jigs* was too small to be the sole offering, and the spring selection was not sent out until summer because of the need to combine the two books. The *Anglican Digest* boasted that a selection of the club was on the current list of best sellers and was available at the Christ Church Book Shop in Little Rock.[107] Prior to the summer mailing of the book club selection, the *Episcopalian*, based in Philadelphia but no longer in press, began publishing excerpts of essays from *O Ye Jigs & Juleps!* in its June 1962 issue.

Also in June, the *Crowell-Collier Newsletter* echoed and added to the accolades of *Newsweek* and the *New York Times Book Review* with the article "Hallelujah, Glory Three Times and Amen, Macmillan Publishes 1904 Literary Gem":

> Thanks to a pair of sharp-eyed Macmillan employees, a bookshop owner, an Episcopal Bishop's wife, a family pastor and the late author's daughter, an enchanting group of essays has found its way into print after nearly a 60-year wait.
>
> Written by a 10-year-old Southern girl named Virginia Cary Hudson for her teacher back in 1904, the collection was published by Macmillan on April 16 in a little book called *O Ye Jigs & Juleps!* In it, Virginia makes some humorous but penetrating observations of life in a sleepy Kentucky town in

the early 1900's, setting down her impressions of such things as school, the library and everlasting life ("God gives it to you, and you can't get rid of it.").

The essays were discovered after the author's death in 1954 by her daughter, Virginia Cleveland Mayne, who found them in an attic trunk and took them to the family pastor. He brought them to Mrs. Angus Dun, wife of the Episcopal Bishop of Washington, D.C. Mrs. Dun, in turn, showed them to Martha Johnson, co-owner with Doris Thompson of Washington's Francis Scott Key Bookshop and literary agency, who began to look for a publisher. That's when Macmillan entered the picture.

Mrs. Johnson asked James R. Gregg, Macmillan's eastern regional sales manager, to read the essays. "When I saw them," says Jim, "I knew they had to be published, so I brought them right up to our New York office." Macmillan, in the person of Editor Betty Bartelme, took a good look at Virginia's highly original slice of life and agreed with Jim. As a result, Macmillan published what turned out to be a bestseller. (On May 27, *O Ye Jigs & Juleps!* made the *New York Times Book Review*'s Best Seller List for the first time.) The book is already in its fifth printing, bringing the total number of copies in print to 45,000.

Critics too have fallen in love with Virginia's book. According to Lewis Nichols of the *New York Times Book Review*, "Delightful is the word for it, whoever you are." ...

Jim Gregg is especially proud of the gracious thank you note he received from Virginia's daughter for his part in bringing the essays to the public.

"It was your faith that took *O Ye Jigs & Juleps!* to Macmillan," Mrs. Mayne writes.

"I truly feel that the angels knew exactly the person, the time and the place ... It was on the Monday before Easter in 1954, that I left my mother in a cemetery in Kentucky; and it is the Monday before Easter in 1962 that Macmillan says is our publication date. How the Good Lord has worked it out, even unto the letter of the day. Thank you very much."

A photo accompanies the story in the *Crowell Collier Newsletter*. The caption reads, "Something to Smile About: Without help from (l. to r.) Martha Johnson, Jim Gregg and Virginia Mayne, *O Ye Jigs & Juleps!* might still be resting in an attic trunk." The *Newsletter* captured the spirit of jubilation behind the successful book, but it overlooked the fire that burned the attic trunk in 1952 and my mother's work since 1954.

My mother sent numerous copies of the book to people she hoped would be interested. Walt Disney responded with a personal letter dated July 12, 1962, with praises for *O Ye Jigs & Juleps!* Expressing gratitude for her thoughtfulness, he said that he knew he was going to enjoy having the book in his library. Sir Alec Guinness, the famous actor, wrote to my mother on July 5, 1964, from 300 Central Park West:

Thank you so much for *O Ye Jigs & Juleps!* I had never read it, though had heard it of course, and goodness me, what a delight it is. And it has brought back to memory vividly and nonsensically my Anglican Episcopalian days. I shall treasure it and can't wait for friends in England to read it.[108]

By August 26, 1962, my parents' wedding anniversary, *O Ye Jigs & Juleps!* occupied the third place on the *New York Times* Best Sellers list and had appeared on the list for fourteen weeks. Running neck and neck with *O Ye Jigs & Juleps!* in the third and fourth positions on the list for at least four weeks was Barbara

Tuchman's *The Guns of August*, published in 1962 and awarded the Pulitzer Prize in 1963.

The scrapbook that my mother assembled for recording the story of publishing *O Ye Jigs & Juleps!* contains numerous other clippings from newspapers—reviews, local best-seller lists, and serialized selections from *O Ye Jigs & Juleps!* in the *Cleveland Press*, the *Courier Journal*, the *Miami Herald*, the *Washington Daily News*, and other newspapers.[109] The *Courier Journal* serialized the best seller beginning March 3, 1963.[110] The *Cleveland Press* serialized some chapters as well and launched their appearance with a contest for young ladies. Ten-year-olds were invited to describe in a letter the most amusing experience of their lives. The *Press* promised to print the ten best letters and award ten dollars to each of the ten winners.[111] Some articles in the scrapbook are missing the publication's title and the date; others fortunately were protected by the original envelope in which they were mailed or have a certification from a press bureau. C. C. Hartley in his column, "The Spectator," advised quickly, "If you want to relax and forget the worldly troubles that beset you take time off to read the Macmillan Company's new book by Virginia Cary Hudson ... It will evoke laughs that will do you good."[112] A reviewer for the *Chicago Heights Star* on April 19, 1962, called *O Ye Jigs & Juleps!*, "an exquisitely printed and illustrated little book that is a riot from beginning to end ... It could become a classic record of a child's unabashed view of God and man."

The windy city gave *O Ye Jigs & Juleps!* a positive review in the May 20, 1962, *Chicago Sunday Tribune* "Magazine of Books": "Trenchant Precocity from an Old Attic Trunk" by Ethel Jacobson, a freelance writer. Jacobson called it "a lollypop of a book" and highlighted the fight Virginia had with a girl from the Campbellite church over the custom of wearing hats to church. When the girl said, "Fooie on St. Paul," Virginia slapped her "for the whole state of Christ's church universal" and pinched her "for herself." Jacobson observed, "Of all the theological schisms that historically have riven the church, few have been stated so directly or resolved so swiftly." My mother wrote to express her gratitude to Ethel Jacobson, as she did to others. Jacobson replied on June 28, 1962, from Bishop, California,[113] and enclosed a cutting from a letter written by friends of hers who had loved *O Ye Jigs & Juleps!* Jacobson wished for more information about Virginia, as did many others, whose desire to know more moved my mother to start writing "Ah, Dear Readers."[114]

Many envelopes in the scrapbook are marked with the date that my mother replied to the letters of appreciation that she received. The writer of a letter dated October 6, 1962, exclaimed:

> *O Ye Jigs & Juleps!* arrived yesterday, and I could not wait until I had delved into it at least for a brief peek. Soon my friends and fellow workers were rushing in to learn why I was shrieking with merriment in spite of the doleful fact of other workers being laid low with colds and therefore piles of things to be worried about, etc., etc. But no worries for me just then—I was thoroughly en rapport with Virginia, who talks language which I understand and feels things in which I share.

The same writer answered my mother's letter and explained her enthusiasm for the little book: "Virginia, you see, was in my generation. I was born in 1901, so that she and I were no doubt in Sunday School during much of the same period. She said so honestly so many of the things which I thought, so rebelliously, or impishly, or wonderingly. How I wish I had known her."[115]

Not all readers of *O Ye Jigs & Juleps!* were endeared to the book, however. I remember my mother's distress when calls came in from the Francis Scott Key Bookshop alerting her to the dogged presence of a representative of *Time* magazine, who asserted that he would remain at the bookshop until he proved that *O Ye Jigs & Juleps!* was a fake. He went away without gathering evidence for his case. The magazine published a review on August 3, 1962. My grandmother's name was given incorrectly in the review title as Virginia Gary Hudson, and her childhood residence was wrongly listed as Louisville, not Versailles:

Last year's flyweight bestseller was *Winnie Ille Pu*, a Latin translation of A.A. Milne's wonderful beary story. Almost no one could read it, but it sold awfully well (it looked impressive on the coffee table, and the English original made a dandy pony). The book that seems certain to be this year's small mad success is not written in Latin, and it is not really a children's book. But it is, or is claimed to be, a child's book. *O Ye Jigs & Juleps!*, a sheaf of very severe, very funny essays about adult nonsense, shows the world of Louisville as it was seen in 1904 by ten-year-old Virginia Cary Hudson, then a pupil in an Episcopal boarding school. Its publishers say, word of honor, that it is Virginia's work, discovered decades later in an attic trunk by her daughter. The story is that the little Virginia stammered, and her English teacher allowed her to write out her assignments.

Whatever the case, *Jigs* does not quite have the ring of authenticity achieved by that small classic *The Young Visiters*, supposedly written at the turn of the century by nine-year-old Daisy Ashford. Nevertheless, *Jigs* makes some of the best out-loud reading since the original *Pooh*.

The review author then quoted from the essay on sacraments and a few other passages, concluding that Virginia "is a properly brought up little girl, and she ends every chapter with a prayer." The Benedicite verse that gave the book its title closed the review. Thus the reviewer, who had challenged the authenticity of my grandmother's authorship, did not find a way to deny it and ended up recognizing the book's value.

On the heels of the book's success, interesting and sometimes inaccurate claims emerged about characters in the book and about Virginia's identity. A man once ran excitedly into the Francis Scott Key Bookshop, exclaiming that he was little Melvin, the boy whom Virginia baptized in the rain barrel.[116] Little Melvin surfaced and identified himself in Louisville as well. A short article from San Diego presented a false memory not of Melvin but of Virginia herself. Stuart Lake, a writer from that city, remembered her as a beautiful newspaperwoman:

> Virginia Cary Hudson, the 10-year-old puckish author of "O Ye Jigs & Juleps!", which is currently being published in the Evening Tribune, was a contemporary of San Diego writer Stuart Lake, an ex-New York newspaperman. Virginia's essays were written nearly 60 years ago, and forgotten, but she is remembered by Lake as the most beautiful newspaperwoman he ever met, and one of the best in New York. "She wasn't a sob sister, and she didn't trade on her feminine lure," Lake says, "and that was in the pre-World War I era when few women were offered newspaper jobs."

Lake understood Virginia's character, but she was never in New York! Stuart N. Lake was born (1889) in Rome, New York, and wrote material for various westerns; he gained fame for his biography of Wyatt Earp, the basis of a movie and a television series.[117] He died in San Diego in 1964. It seems likely that he is the same Stuart Lake who thought he remembered Virginia as a New York newspaperwoman.

Another newspaper clipping from Southern California, undated but probably published in October 1962, reported that the actor Robert Young spoke to the women's club of Carlsbad, California, at a luncheon with tables "decorated with a Halloween theme." He explained that he was going to give a reading to the group and said, "I struggled for several years to write speeches and give them before deciding that actors are not equipped to do anything but mimic and make faces in front of a camera." He then read three chapters from *O Ye Jigs & Juleps!*: "Sacraments," "Etiquette in Church," and "Everlasting Life." He stated, "I find it refreshing and healthy to examine the world, people, and attitudes through the vision of a child." The article reported that the actor's "pleasure in the book was obvious throughout and came across to a spellbound audience." It further noted that all four daughters of the Young family attended an Episcopal school, the Bishop's School in La Jolla.

The fame of *O Ye Jigs & Juleps!* not only reached the West Coast but also extended across the Atlantic to Ireland, England, Holland, and Switzerland. The *Church of Ireland Gazette* reviewed the book in its July 27, 1962, issue, first providing background on the essays and the role of Bishop Dun's wife in finding a publisher. The reviewer called *O Ye Jigs & Juleps!* a "delightfully entertaining book, one that will transform the wintriest of summer days." On Virginia's personality and character, the writer remarked,

> Virginia never sat chewing the end of her pencil. She tackled the weightiest subject with gay abandon revealing as the words tumbled out a lively sense of everyday participation in holy things and a life brimming over with religious joy. There were no half measures about Virginia ... the reader feels sorry that more of her chatter-on-paper has not been preserved in that attic trunk where these 'masterpieces of childhood' were discovered.

The *Sunday Times* (London) reviewed the little book in early November 1963. A friend of my mother's saw the review in Paris on November 10, clipped it, and mailed it to my mother.[118] The British Broadcasting Corporation featured the reading of two brief extracts from *O Ye Jigs & Juleps!* in its program "The First Day of the Week" on May 12 and 26, 1974.[119] A Dutch edition of the little book, *O Gij Polka's en Perendrups*, appeared in 1963.[120] The Swiss *Die Weltwoche* printed a shortened version of the book in April 1966, including the essays on the sacraments, church etiquette, and the library. In 1966, a German edition of the little book, translated by Peter Motram, was published in Switzerland. The title was simply *Virginia* (Bern: Benteli, 1966), and it included illustrations by Hanny Fries. In 1968–1969, my sister-in-law Margaret's sixth grade class in the Panama Canal Zone featured *O Ye Jigs & Juleps!* on the reading list. Margaret was proud to know the author of one of the 204 books she read that year.

The book's title caused confusion at least once, and its readability aided a student plagiarist. According to a note in the *Saturday Review* on November 17, 1962, a person asked for *O Ye Jigs & Juleps!* in Littleton, New Hampshire, and the bookstore said it did not stock bartender books. From California the author of a college composition workbook wrote to my mother apologizing for the mistaken publication of an essay from *O Ye Jigs & Juleps!* as a piece of student writing. One of the professor's students had turned in a copy of "Etiquette at Church" as his or her own work, and the instructor had included it in a published collection of student writing, considering it "certainly the best in the book." She had even read the paper to other classes as an example of the kind of writing she "would have liked for them to do." She herself had not read *O Ye Jigs & Juleps!*, although she had given it as a Christmas gift to her niece.[121]

The short and lively essays from *O Ye Jigs & Juleps!* lend themselves well to reading aloud in various settings, from the classroom to BBC broadcasts, and there are now versions on YouTube.[122] Not long after publication, Rebecca (Becky) Scott began doing dramatic readings from *O Ye Jigs & Juleps!* for church and other small audiences in Michigan. She and my mother corresponded for years. I recently came upon a letter and a photo that Becky sent to my mother in 1983. Becky wrote, "I certainly have enjoyed all the notes, news clippings and letters from you. If anything outstanding and exciting happens regarding your books, I hope you'll let me know." Becky now awaits news from me on publishing my mother's story. E-mail links us, as do letters and the telephone. In July 2014, Becky did two readings of *O Ye Jigs & Juleps!* in Alaska, where her sister lives.[123]

Several people wrote screenplays based on *O Ye Jigs & Juleps!* and proposed them to my mother. Someone wanted to model an *O Ye Jigs & Juleps!* play on *You're A Good Man, Charlie Brown*. I remember going to New York with my parents to see *Charlie Brown* so that we could get an idea of what my grandmother's character would be like in such a play. The early attempts at screenplays based on *O Ye Jigs & Juleps!* were not successful. Eventually, Don Musselman proposed a play set to music composed by Sim Broadfield. I was handling the book's copyright then and gave Mr. Musselman permission to proceed.[124] His delightful musical was published in 1992, and we enjoyed some years of very pleasant correspondence and telephone conversations. Another proposal for a stage adaptation of *O Ye Jigs & Juleps!* arrived two months before my mother's death. When I told the author about Mr. Musselman's play, she suggested we explore movie possibilities instead.[125] The last I heard, she was not able to procure funding for her project.

My mother received many invitations to speak at events, from women's club luncheons to church groups to book signings with the authors of other best-selling books. The best-selling authors of 1962 and 1963 included Anne Morrow Lindbergh, William Faulkner, Barbara Tuchman, Louis Nizer, James Baldwin, J. D. Salinger, Morris West, Fletcher Knebel, Charles W. Bailey II, John Steinbeck, Bruce Catton, Charles M. Schulz, and Betty Friedan. I remember hearing my mother rehearse downstairs in her study what she was going to say at the book discussions. She made lists of rare words, definitions, place names, and whatever else she might need to consult at a moment's notice. When I look back at the people she was meeting in the bookstores of the early sixties, I understand the nervousness she felt and why she spent so many hours practicing before her talks. When I began giving academic lectures at conferences, I too practiced them, and I felt that her spirit occupied the rehearsal space with me.

The notes my mother typed for the many book talks she gave grew into the pages of "Ah, Dear Readers." In her scrapbook I found clippings from a talk given at the Naval Academy women's club event (no date) and another from the St. Louis *Globe Democrat*, dated October 29, 1964. In St. Louis she addressed a luncheon meeting during the General Convention of the Episcopal Church, an event she and my father had often attended as interested spectators or elected delegates. The audience asked questions about the impact of success on daily life, and my mother replied that, like the comedian Phyllis Diller, she was "17 years behind on ironing." She also remarked that my father and I were faring well, that we were "all on the treadmill together," and that I had even learned to cook.[126] That I do not recall, but perhaps it was the beginning of my efforts at frying frozen breaded shrimp—the only thing I remember "cooking" before I was married. When the *Globe Democrat* story appeared, the second book of Virginia's writings, *Credos & Quips*, had just been published. The account of its publication and that of *Close Your Eyes When Praying* and *Flapdoodle, Trust & Obey* did not fit into the *O Ye Jigs & Juleps!* scrapbook my mother made. Neither did many memorabilia from the book-signing events, which grew to include two, three, and then four books, with *O Ye Jigs & Juleps!* overshadowing the others. Back home in Kentucky, recognition for Virginia Cary Hudson and her writings grew. On Sunday, October 3, 1965, the St. James Court Association dedicated a plaque at 1453 St. James Court, where Virginia had lived until her death in 1954.[127] My mother attended the dedication, which took place within the association's annual art show. In July 1967, the Sacajawea Festival in Cloverport, Kentucky, featured guided tours stopping at three historic sites: the place where Abraham Lincoln and his family crossed the Ohio River on their way to Indiana; the grave of Virginia Cary Hudson, the author of *O Ye Jigs & Juleps!*; and the home of Joseph Holt, who prosecuted the accused murderers of President Lincoln.

By July 8, 1990, about a year after my mother died, Virginia Cary Hudson's name and the little book's title were well enough known that completing column 15 in the *Washington Post Magazine*'s crossword puzzle required two words from the book's title. The puzzle provided the clue "__ __ *Jigs & Juleps!*, Virginia C. Hudson." The *Kentucky Encyclopedia* (1992) includes an entry on Virginia Cary Hudson,[128] and alongside photos of 1453 St. James Court, David Dominé remarks in *Old Louisville* (2013) that "Virginia Cary Hudson was probably the most famous resident of the house."[129] In this age of the Internet, Virginia Cary Hudson appears on YouTube, Wikipedia, and Amazon.com. A group of scholars at the University of North Alabama is now studying the literary influences on Virginia's writing and planning a scholarly edition of *O Ye Jigs & Juleps!* Glory three times also and amen twice!

Publishing Virginia's Adult Writings

My mother recognized the extraordinary role that my grandmother played as a preaching teacher at her Episcopal church and as an invited preacher to Louisville's nondenominational chapels. My mother knew that the two hundred–some letters that her mother wrote to her showed the same exceptional faith, exuberance, and sense of humor that radiated from the religious talks. The captivating stories, whether Kentucky tales or retellings of biblical episodes, reveal my grandmother's gift for empathetic, humorous, and lively storytelling. She created a universe populated by people living in her world as well as by historical and biblical figures. God and the angels watched over all; daily behavior and eternal reward were inseparable.

How would my mother publish my grandmother's adult writings? Challenges to Virginia Cary Hudson's genuineness strengthened my mother's resolve. A five-by-eight index card records the landmarks in my mother's quest to publish my grandmother's adult writings. My mother typed the key dates of the process and remarked on the same card that she "had religious adult writings ready, as [she] knew the essays would be popular." Virginia Cary Hudson Cleveland's adult writings included many compositions, far beyond the sixty-five printed pages of *Credos & Quips*. My mother outlined, listed, and numbered the contents of a potential third volume of my grandmother's writings that would contain the remainder of the religious essays along with my grandmother's letters to my mother and to me, notes for talks, poems, essays, fables, drawings, my scrapbook with the title "Sitting and Thinking," and even more. The book that my mother planned would use my scrapbook's title.

Behind the publishing activity, a painful conflict arose between my mother and some members of her family over publishing the writings. A brief agreement in the early 1960s had granted her a release to publish the essays in *O Ye Jigs & Juleps!* However, by early 1963, a Kentucky attorney had been hired to demand, under threat of a lawsuit, a full accounting for the royalties and an agreement that would allow her family full participation in marketing the book. My mother felt betrayed by her family's challenges and lack of gratitude. She reluctantly hired a lawyer and an accountant to handle her affairs. In the end, the law supported my mother. She had in fact been awarding herself less than she was owed according to common business practices. She was due reimbursement because she had not allowed for her own expenses and had overpaid the others' shares of the royalties. The Kentucky attorney finally resigned, because the royalties and thus his share were not turning out to be as high as he had been led to believe.

Even before the family strife, my mother was exhausted from the requirements of handling a best seller—defending the book's authenticity, making appearances, taking phone calls, writing letters, and more. Her eyes were bothered by fatigue and nervousness, and her doctors recommended a complete change, that she go away for a significant amount of time and leave the book business behind her. At last, from late February to late April 1963, she set sail on the *Empress of Canada* and enjoyed the trip that she and her mother had dreamed of making together. She took copies of *O Ye Jigs & Juleps!* with her and proudly held one up for photos. Aboard a camel in Egypt, she held the book in her lap and recaptured the joy at her achievement.

Virginia Cleveland Mayne riding a camel in Egypt while holding O Ye Jigs & Juleps!, *March 1963*

A letter that I wrote my mother from boarding school in Kentucky just before she left conveyed my excitement about the upcoming trip and the camel ride. I told her to send lots of postcards and warned her not to fall off the camel. However, a Kentucky horsewoman was not intimidated by getting on a camel! My letters both before and after the trip voiced anger and worry about the legal contention and its effects on my mother's health. It is clear to me some fifty years later that I wanted desperately to be at home. I did not return to the Kentucky school in the fall of 1963. That is a story unto itself.

From December 1962 to November 1963, she waited for clearance of the rights to publish the first volume, *Credos & Quips* (1964), as well as the letters that her mother had written her. Once an agreement was signed in June 1963, *Credos & Quips* moved to publication. A March 27, 1964, letter from the Macmillan Company accompanied the galleys and requested their return by April 2! The schedule called for presenting the book at the American Booksellers Association (ABA) convention on June 8, 1964. The cover picture and illustrations for *Credos & Quips* again featured Karla Kuskin's delightful drawings. The artist linked *Credos & Quips* to *O Ye Jigs & Juleps!* by juxtaposing drawings of Virginia as a child and as an adult.

An advertisement from the *New York Times* featured a young Virginia strolling up the Best Sellers list while an adult Virginia teaches a class. The book's publicity stressed continuity. As a monthly book trade publication stated, "As an adult, she retains both her honesty and her funniness ... Her words will leave her readers, as they left her hearers, heartily laughing, but better than they were before."[130]

Credos & Quips often appeared in reviews of *Flapdoodle* that looked back on the preceding books. The *Dallas Morning News* (Tuesday, October 27, 1964) reported on an autographing session that the Cokesbury Book Store sponsored there the preceding day. The story, "'Ghost Writer' Is No Spook In World of Literary Haunts," recounted the success of *O Ye Jigs & Juleps!* before announcing that, "the late Virginia Cary Hudson's daughter has done it again with 'Credos & Quips,' drawn from her mother's talks before Episcopal church women in Louisville, Ky." The article continued, "The second Virginia's aims in assembling the second book were again 'to pass on the wonderment' of her remarkable parent's humor, good sense and piety—and 'to prove that Virginia was as fabulous in the last year of her life as when she was 10.'"

A Macmillan editor suggested that my mother consider making a trip through the South, including Dallas, after her stay in St. Louis, where she attended the triennial convention of the Protestant Episcopal Church.[131] As the *Dallas Morning News* reported, "There, to her awe and astonishment, she shared billing at an autographing session with California's famous Bishop James Pike." By 1964 Bishop Pike had gained national attention for his support of racial desegregation, his avant-garde opinions on the ordination of women, and his outspoken challenges to key tenets of Christian doctrine. In 1965, Bishop Pike declared the Reverend Phyllis Edwards a first-order deacon more than a decade before women were ordained as transitional deacons or priests in the Episcopal Church (1977).[132] The account from Dallas continued, "As always, she wished for her mother's presence. 'If they could have seen the real person, Bishop Pike would have known that day that there was somebody else in the room.'" I recall that my mother objected to Bishop Pike's challenges to the Trinity. She told him after the book session that she did not agree with him on that. The Dallas story finished with observations on the long road to publishing *O Ye Jigs & Juleps!*: "Mrs. Mayne already had collected wall-to-wall rejection slips by then, mailing out the essay collection 'as if there were no tomorrow.'" The article ended with a memorable saying from my grandmother, concluding that my mother "must also have heeded her mother's words: 'Take a firm grip on the handle of prayer, and open the door'" (*Credos*, 64).

Before St. Louis and Dallas, Mother spoke at book signings in Birmingham, Alabama, and Nashville, Tennessee. A newspaper article from Birmingham, Alabama (Sunday, October 18, 1964), announced, "Noted author will make visit here," implying that my mother was the book's author. However pleased she would have been at the enthusiastic tone of the story, she was unhappy with the mistaken idea that she was the author of her mother's writings.

In Birmingham, she spoke at a tea from 3:30–5:00 p.m. in the tea room of Loveman's Department Store (closed in 1980), the scene of civil rights protests in 1963 against the store's hiring practices and segregated lunch counter.[133] Immediately following the book signing there, she headed to Nashville and then St. Louis and Dallas.

The practical demands of publishing and promotional appearances required setting limits on the material for future publication. After *Credos & Quips*, my mother decided to focus on the letters that my grandmother had written to her. Editing my grandmother's letters posed significant challenges. How would my mother assemble in a meaningful way undated letters, multiple letters written the same day, and pairs of letters that my grandmother wrote to my mother and to me and placed in the same envelope? How would my mother capture and preserve the essence of her mother's character and wit? How would she protect the identity of people named in the letters? Extensive notes, lists, and cross-references mark numbered copies of the letters and the folders containing them. In 1963, my mother began reading and editing the letters that her mother had written to her and to me. The letters cover more than a decade of events, from my mother's move to Washington, DC, in 1946 to my grandmother's death in April 1954. According to my mother's notes, she read and organized letters from April to November 1963, and on her birthday, November 21, the same year, she started to edit the letters. The editing involved a complicated process of historical reconstruction.

My mother submitted a full manuscript for the letters to Macmillan at the end of September 1964. From the lists and dates she made on the folder covers, it seems that she wanted to publish selected letters to her and to me in chronological order. She contextualized the correspondence in a narrative to provide a framework for the letters, the events, and the people involved. Some of the pages in "Ah, Dear Readers" belong to this narrative framework. Looking at the sheer quantity of my mother's careful notes and ordering, I wonder how she managed to accomplish that much work when the success of *O Ye Jigs & Juleps!* placed heavy demands on her time.

Rejection stood in my mother's path again. A letter dated January

15, 1965, arrived at the Francis Scott Key Bookshop with the news that Macmillan had rejected the manuscript of my grandmother's letters. My mother learned of the negative response in person when she went to the bookshop on January 29, 1965. *Credos & Quips* had done well, according to the letter, but it had garnered few reviews. Macmillan had sent out just over 52,500 copies of *Credos & Quips* by January 1965. The sales (disappointing to Macmillan), the small number of reviews, and a feeling that the proposed volume would not appeal to a wide readership led to the rejection. The editor's last sentence expressed the hope "that Virginia's feelings will not be hurt." They were, but she was not defeated. In late June 1965, Harper & Row issued a contract for the letters. My mother and I learned of it in Copenhagen, during the North Cape cruise that we took to celebrate my graduation from high school. Martha and Doris, her agents, signed the new agreement on July 8 in Washington, DC.

During a visit to Louisville and apparently in front of 1453 St. James Court, my grandmother's former home, my mother announced the forthcoming publication of *Flapdoodle, Trust & Obey*. Her undated, handwritten note reads,

> It is a great privilege and pleasure to come home today and I want to thank those who have made this "Glory three times also and Amen twice" event possible. The road that led to the publication of *O Ye Jigs & Juleps!* was a long and hard one, finally accomplished in April of 1962. Two years later and from April to September, *Credos & Quips*, written in this house, was published. I cannot think of a more apt place or time to announce the coming of a third book of my mother's writings— Virginia's letters to be entitled, *Flapdoodle, Trust & Obey*.

Publication of the letters was in progress on February 15, 1966, when Barbara Walters interviewed my mother on the *Today Show*. The *TV Guide* for that day reads, "Mrs. Lewis H. Mayne discusses *Flapdoodle, Trust & Obey*, a book of letters to her by her mother." I remember the awe of seeing my mother on the television screen.

There she was with Barbara Walters, the television personality and broadcast journalist! My father and I could not restrain our tears. Memories of the long road to publication swelled over us: the envelopes with returned manuscripts, my mother at her typewriter, the first contract from Macmillan, my mother rehearsing her talks, *O Ye Jigs & Juleps!* reaching the *New York Times* Best Sellers list, and now a live appearance from New York on national television.

Harper Religious Books announced in early 1966 the coming of "another Bestseller from a pen dipped in magic." The announcement appealed to the readers who delighted in *O Ye Jigs & Juleps!*: "Millions of Americans can testify to the enchantment of Virginia Cary Hudson's *O Ye Jigs & Juleps!*, a collection of essays written when she was a precocious ten-year old."[134] The Seabury Bookstore and Harper & Row invited guests to an autographing party at 815 Second Avenue, New York City, on February 17, 1966, the day of publication. My mother must have been thrilled at an event that took place in the building that housed the headquarters of the Episcopal Church for so many years. However, she was surprised when she learned the title and saw some of the publicity written by Harper & Row, as well as the edited letters themselves. Harper & Row had hired an editor to arrange and edit the materials, from the letters published in *Flapdoodle* to the Sunday talks that followed in *Close Your Eyes When Praying*, for which a contract was issued in 1968. Out of the two hundred some letters that my grandmother wrote, this editor constructed eighteen texts for *Flapdoodle, Trust & Obey*. As a result, several of the eighteen texts combine more than one original letter, up to four actually. After checking the letter files, I found that the first letter in *Flapdoodle* combines three original pieces: one describing Virginia's meeting an old beau, a second telling the true story of a cousin who made a disastrous move to the country, and the third reporting an overheard conversation with a funny description of my grandmother. My mother previously combined some material as well in order to eliminate passages with private information. Her notes include a photocopy of *Flapdoodle*'s published table of contents that she annotated with her own system of numbering for the letters, as they appeared in the manuscript that she submitted and that was not returned to her.

My grandmother wrote to my mother most often as "Dear Brat," in a joking tone that becomes evident after reading repeated assurances that my mother, unlike her other children, had never caused her worry. In fact, the contract that my mother signed with Harper & Row cited the book's title as "Dear Brat," and the change on the published book to *Flapdoodle, Trust & Obey* took my mother by surprise. The original letters close with "Love, Mother" or "Love," often followed by a picture. The editors selected a uniform closing to the letters, "Love, Little Mama," which my grandmother did not use, and they honed down her many forms of address to a limited number of phrases, such as "My Little Plum."

My grandmother often drew herself with a sketch that reflected her feelings—happy, angry, sad, tired. Those could be different

A typical rapid signature from Virginia on a postcard: "Love, Mother"

A drawing of an unhappy face that closes a letter

A drawing of Virginia with new earrings that closes a letter

if events changed her day. Shown are several examples of my grandmother's various signatures, including a quickly signed postcard to my mother, sent from the post office; a letter that closes with an unhappy face; and a letter that closes with a drawing reflecting her excitement over some new earrings. "Devil whispering in one ear, an angel in the other. That's me."

The editorial selection of writings for publication left the letters without any framework to contextualize events. More seriously, standardizing forms of address and signatures narrowed my grandmother's creativity of expression. Furthermore, the publicity generated a major misconception, namely that my grandmother was a widow who struggled to make a living by hoping to sell her writings and by running a boardinghouse.

However, the publisher's advertising for *Flapdoodle* stressed its continuity with *O Ye Jigs & Juleps!*, a theme that won my mother's approval. Reviewers, nonetheless, differ on whether or not *Flapdoodle* constituted a sequel to *Jigs*. Lewis Nichols, who had praised *O Ye Jigs & Juleps!* in the *New York Times Book Review,* announced the publication of *Flapdoodle* in his column, "In and Out of Books," on February 27, 1966, under the heading, "Sequel."

> There arrived from Harper & Row the other day— its religious department—a slim little book entitled "Flapdoodle, Trust & Obey," the author, Virginia Cary Hudson. It is set down as a sequel to "O Ye Jigs & Juleps!" also a slim little book which back in 1962 and '63 was on everyone's bestseller list, and since publication has had sales of over 390,000 copies, hard-cover alone. "Jigs" contained the reflections of a 10-year-old Virginia; "Flapdoodle" contains letters written by the mature Virginia to her grown daughter, Virginia Cleveland Mayne in Washington.

Anne Hitch of the *Baltimore Sun* did not consider *Flapdoodle* a sequel: "To call this collection of letters from mama a sequel to the genteelly rollicking 'O Ye Jigs & Juleps!' of the best-seller list a few years ago is hardly fair to the reader expecting more of the same from the precocious author of the first book."[135] In contrast, E. D. Witherspoon with "Now, Flapdoodle" (*Presbyterian Survey*, Atlanta, GA, August 1966) exclaimed that "Flapdoodle, Trust & Obey by Virginia Cary Hudson ... is a worthy sequel to O Ye Jigs & Juleps!" Likewise, Abigail Fenwick in the *Birmingham News* affirmed the value of *Flapdoodle*: "This is marvelous reading in the tradition of *O Ye Jigs & Juleps!* The author is the same and the quality and popularity of this effort should also remain the same." Furthermore, Fenwick vouched for the book as "entertainment, plain and simple." She recommended, "There is a great deal packed in this little book which might be put to good use on one of those gloomy days when everything looks grim as the grave."

Some reviewers disagreed. In the *Minneapolis Tribune* on February 20, 1966, Lora Lee Watson claimed, "Flapdoodle Isn't Worth Half a Jig and Julep."

> You who found "O Ye Jigs & Juleps" a delight a few years ago will be interested to know that its author is again in print. But you're almost certain to be disappointed if you expect another "Jigs." "Flapdoodle" is twice as long and not half as appealing or entertaining.
>
> "Jigs" was supposed to have been written by Virginia at age 10. "Flapdoodle" is made up of letters to her daughter, written when she was a grandmother. There's wit—but much of it lacks sparkle and spontaneity.
>
> And there's something about letters that start with such endearments as "My Little Plum," "My Little Butterfly" and "My Little Hummingbird" and are signed "Little Mama" that induces in at least this one reader a tendency to nausea.

Watson apparently reacted negatively to the uniform signature and similar forms of address that the editor and publisher chose. How might the editing have affected Watson's conclusion that "some of the other letters even have a glimmer of the charm of the earlier Virginia. But just a glimmer." I also wonder if her remark that, "'Jigs' was supposed to have been written by Virginia at age 10," reveals a skepticism toward the letters' authenticity and therefore their merit.

A book-signing event on February 16, 1966, featured my mother at the Sheraton-Cleveland Hotel with noted newspaperwoman and author Adela Rogers St. John, whose *Tell No Man* was released in 1966, and with Theodore Sorensen, special counsel to President John F. Kennedy, who had published *Kennedy* with Harper & Row in 1965. In the *Pittsburgh Press* on February 20, 1966, Charlotte Cheney proclaimed *Flapdoodle* a success: "Juleps Sequel a Smash: Mama's Back with Delightful Wit, Wisdom." She told her readers to celebrate the coming book: "Dance a jig and ice the juleps in anticipation of Virginia Cary Hudson's 'Flapdoodle, Trust & Obey,' a sequel to the little book that lately delighted readers while it filled the coffers of book stores across the nation." Cheney described my grandmother as an "adventurous soul," who wrote with an "energetic style." She observed that "Mama could make even dusting high adventure. On ordinary, dull days, she used a plain old turkey feather duster. But when she feels gay and romantic, out comes the bull's tail duster she bought in Mexico City." She also commented on a favorite theme of my grandmother's: "The world is full of people who aren't doing one thing for anybody."

Two days after Cheney's review appeared, Sydney Van Lear Upshaw, a past president of Virginia Press Women, published "Letters Tell of a Mother's Simple Faith" (*Richmond Times Dispatch*, Tuesday, February 22, 1966). My mother, she said, had just visited Miller & Rhoads the previous day to autograph books. Van Lear Upshaw included some of Mother's remarks and explained the term *flapdoodle*: "'Flapdoodle' is just so much nonsense. But it was descriptive enough for things pertaining to whimsical chatter—or ideas—to have been used by Mark Twain in Huckleberry Finn."[136] The review noted, "The childlike hope in O Ye Jigs & Juleps! persists in the ramblings of the adult Virginia Hudson." In Virginia's accounts of interactions with people whose lives she touched, said Van Lear Upshaw, "involved often was pathos, but the underlying tone was always that hope would win out." Indeed, hope in this world and hope for the next emerge from my grandmother's writings all her life.

Many other announcements and reviews for *Flapdoodle, Trust & Obey* appeared the month of publication. In the *Richmond News Leader*, Dayton Kohler heralded the forthcoming publication with the article title "Observations on Life: Old Fashioned Grace Marks Brief Letters" (February 10, 1966). Patricia McCormack, writing for *United Press International*, chose the captivating title "Woman to Woman: Ma Preached,"[137] for her preview of *Flapdoodle*. McCormack's review was taken up by other newspapers with slight modifications to the title. The *State Times* (Baton Rouge, LA) announced on February 18, 1966, "'Jigs, Juleps' Letters Again Put in Book." The *Times of Erie* (PA), declared on February 23, 1966, "Woman to Woman: Mother's Sensible Notes Are Put into Book Form."

The tone of the assessments of *Flapdoodle* changed after an *Associated Press* review from Miles A. Smith, "Grandma's Advice Is Zesty," appeared on February 23, 1966.

> In 1962 a resurrected collection of essays concocted long ago by a precocious 10-year-old girl had a great popularity. The book was called "O Ye Jigs & Juleps!" This little book is from the same author. The switch is that Virginia grew up, married, had a daughter and finally a granddaughter. Her grandmotherly letters to her daughter are reproduced here.
>
> Mrs. Hudson was writing from the roominghouse she ran in Louisville. Her topics included the schoolteaching roomers and their romances, her helping at the church and hospital, her meeting with an old beau, the funeral of Sister Annie, her triumph in a court case, her sympathy for old and

faithful servants, her homely advice on marriage, her insistence on laughing to keep from crying.

Of course the whole business is syrupy; male readers will shudder at the apparition of a busybody brimming over with cuteness. But with all its yesteryear corn, it is such wholesome maize that it would be a shame to overlook its electric zest for living.

The very same review appeared numerous times, in at least thirty newspapers, including ones from Fairbanks, Alaska; Monterrey, California; Sheridan, Wyoming; Nogales, Arizona; Bridgeport, Connecticut; and Key West, Florida.[138] With it the incorrect name of "Mrs. Hudson," instead of Mrs. Cleveland, circulated as well. Reviewers made some changes to the text and to the title of the review, such as "Wholesome Corn" and "Syrupy, but Wholesome." At least one reviewer made the connection between *Flapdoodle* and *O Ye Jigs & Juleps!* obvious in the review's title, "Jigs & Juleps Motif Revived."[139]

Some readers, however, objected to Smith's assessment of the letters as "syrupy." Velma S. Daniels, writing from Florida, found that "the author reveals a genius for speaking for every woman and to every man." Overall, she called the new book "hilarious" and concluded that "we guarantee that you will be sorry when you have finished the last page of this charming little book." Finally, she said to her audience, "and if you have failed to look on the funny side of life—then this book is still for you, for it is a continual fountain of mirth."[140] From the West Coast, Nancy O'Gara agreed somewhat with Smith in observing that the book's "appeal will be greater to women than to men, but it certainly has charm." Her first reaction to the letters was negative ("she felt like saying 'good grief'"), but "she didn't stop reading, and enchantment soon took her over." She found that the letters "reveal a touching and delightful personality, full of love, faith and humor." Unlike most readers, O'Gara had not read *O Ye Jigs & Juleps!*, but she intended to do so after reading *Flapdoodle*.[141]

On May 9, 1966, the Monday after the Kentucky Derby, my mother made an appearance on the WAVE TV morning show in Louisville and then spent the afternoon taping an interview for the same channel. Sharing airtime in her home city with a recap of the Derby weekend must surely have delighted her. In late March 1968, the fourth book, *Close Your Eyes When Praying*, was ready for final review and publication. Harper & Row selected the same editor who had prepared the selection of letters for *Flapdoodle*. The material in *Close Your Eyes When Praying* belonged to the same large collection of writings that my mother had assembled after finishing *O Ye Jigs and Juleps!* What was chosen corresponds to Virginia's Sunday school lessons for the women at Calvary Episcopal Church in Louisville. The lessons were changed to some extent, combining material from more than one place, and descriptive titles were added that do not correspond to the originals. The book's title echoes the words my grandmother used to close the Sunday classes: "Now our prayer. Again I ask you to close your eyes when praying. I do not say, 'Bow your head,' for if I were to bow, my wide-brimmed hat would surely topple to the floor" (*Close Your Eyes*, 69). The classes took place before the main service, and my grandmother frequently referred to Brother Gregory, who rang a bell every week announcing that she had half an hour left before the service started. Apparently she went over time on occasion, and some preferred her classes to the rector's sermon.

In October, an advertisement for *Close Your Eyes When Praying* appeared in *Christian Century*; in November and December, publicity targeted the Christmas market with small ads in the *New York Times Book Review*, *Book World*, the *Atlanta Journal Constitution*, the *Boston Globe*, and the *Los Angeles Times*.[142] The religious writings in *Close Your Eyes When Praying*, as in *Credos & Quips*, received less attention in the press than *Flapdoodle, Trust & Obey*. However, the same remarkable blend of faith, wit, and humor enlivens both *Credos & Quips* and *Close Your Eyes When Praying*, as Virginia reflects on the Bible, tells local stories and personal anecdotes, and preaches strong lessons. The Virginia of *O Ye Jigs and Juleps!* developed an adult voice that retained her sparkling charm, her astute directness, and her lively sense of humor. Her vision, at once down to earth and cosmic, rested on a belief that laced together all her writings. The unity of all my grandmother's works stood out clearly for my mother. My grandmother's views on religion, on studying the Bible, and on women's participation in the church placed her ahead of her time, perhaps further ahead than even her daughter realized.

Chapter 3

Boiling Down Ecclesiastical Double-Talk

My grandmother cut through the fog surrounding complicated Christian doctrine with a sharp pen. She described herself as one who "boils down fancy dressed up ecclesiastical double talk to hellfire and damnation."[143] The same incisive spirit moved her interpretation of the Bible through the eyes of the women characters and through the minds and hearts of female readers. She lamented the lot of Eve and her daughters. In her view, Eve's malignment by theologians and commentators accounted for "countless generations of otherwise relatively sane human beings" having been "bamboozled into believing that the daughters of Eve are the root of all evil" (*Close Your Eyes*, 30).

My grandmother gave talks to several women's groups in Louisville, and she preached at two chapels. She described her manner of speaking when she reacted to a remark from one of the ladies from Calvary Episcopal Church: "Miss So and So, of all people, tells me that I am so charming. Hells Bells! Nobody who boils down fancy dressed up ecclesiastical double talk to hellfire and damnation could be dubbed charming."[144] She also addressed the Little Study Club of Louisville, a group of self-selected women who gathered at the Puritan Hotel and at each other's homes for enrichment, inviting speakers on a range of topics. Finally, she helped the clergy of Louisville during Lent and preached at the Salvation Army Chapel and the Goodwill Chapel, which had services every Tuesday through Thursday plus a three-hour Good Friday service. Virginia also preached on Good Friday at Calvary Episcopal Church. A service leaflet announces the title of her sermon as "Forgiveness and Salvation through the Crucified Lord."[145] Based on the content, the "Four Questions" sermon in *Credos & Quips* is what she delivered to the Calvary Church audience. The full text of her chapel sermons is not extant, but she summarizes a few of them in letters.[146]

The chapters of *Credos & Quips* come from four talks that constitute a coherent collection of teaching on elements of Christian faith. Very little editing was done to the original texts: (1) "The Three Creeds," that is the Apostles' Creed, the Nicene Creed, and the Athanasian Creed;[147] (2) "The Bible," covering the Bible's origins, some early interpreters, and its translation; (3) "The Palms," a reflection on Ash Wednesday and Lent; and (4) "Four Questions," a sermon for Good Friday that raises the questions the Lord will ask on Judgment Day. Interspersed are famous persons and conflicts in church history, humorous anecdotes, prayers—both historical and personal—and the rousing exhortations of a persuasive preacher. The talks published in *Credos & Quips* date from the last years of my grandmother's life. Imagine what and how much more she could have written if she had lived beyond the age of sixty!

The four questions in the Good Friday sermon follow the course of the scriptural reading Matthew 25:35–46 (*Credos*, 43–64). She paraphrases Matthew to pose the first question, "Whom have you seen hungry and thirsty and given food and drink?" She then challenges her listeners directly: "You might want to ask me if I am talking about bums and tramps. If that is what you want to call them, they are exactly those I am talking about. The unfortunate, the victims of circumstances, who are just as much children of God, as we." She goes on to explain spiritual hunger and thirst. Examples of each bring the Bible into the daily life of her listeners. Her second question, based on Matthew 25:36, asks, "Whom have ye seen naked and clothed?" The follow-up statement admonishes her listeners: "There hangs on our rear clothes closet poles enough discarded and seldom used clothing to cover every ragged and shabby person who needs them." As she did for hunger and thirst, my grandmother elaborates on nakedness of other sorts, such as failure that "exposes our woe." The third question picks up Matthew 25:35 and asks, "Whom have you as a stranger taken in?" A forceful exposition follows on what it means to be a stranger: not only one who comes to the door hungry and thirsty but those of different opinions, faith, education, culture, and race. "There are strangers of race, men of different color of skin, whose flesh, and bone, and blood, and feelings are identical with our own," she declares. She adds that there may be strangers in our family whose choices we do not tolerate. Virginia observes, "Sometimes by our words and actions we estrange from ourselves those whom we love the very most." Fourth, my grandmother asks, "Whom have you seen sick and visited in prison?" (Matthew 25:36). She demands how many have visited a prison or tried to do anything about conditions there. Moreover, she continues, those who are sick in mind or imprisoned in spirit also need attention. Virginia reminds her listeners that "there are six other days" than Sunday, "to be lived before we return" to church. The remainder of the sermon offers prayers, citations from scripture, and exhortations to her listeners. The Good Friday service lasted for three hours, with regularly paced scripture readings, prayers, hymns, and periods of quiet. The congregation had plenty to mull over during the silence.

Virginia preached as the Episcopal representative to the Goodwill Chapel in Louisville on multiple occasions. The congregation on any given day could be quite diverse. On an unspecified Monday, she described in a letter her audience the previous week: "Friday, I went to the Goodwill Chapel, which was packed." She began the depiction in language from the King James Bible, "The halt, the lame, and the blind," and continued, "Hoodlum and bum. Catholic, Protestant, and Jew; even the long-haired boys from the House of David. A few ministers, and the Mormon bishop across the street." Members of the House of David, a religious society founded in

Michigan, wore characteristically long hair and beards. Advocates for the health benefits of athletics, the House of David members became widely known through their traveling baseball teams.[148] A few letters relate to my grandmother's Holy Week preaching at the chapel, including Good Friday and, as a separate task, Ash Wednesday and Lent (*Flapdoodle*, 72, 76). Virginia was chosen as the preacher for Good Friday at the Goodwill Chapel during an ecumenical church council meeting in Louisville.[149] The rector of Calvary Episcopal Church was delighted that she was chosen, she reported, but a friend of hers was "dumbfounded," without explanation of why. The friend made sure to attend though. A woman, Baptist or Methodist, challenged Virginia as to whether she was going to make the service denominational, causing Virginia's hair to rise under her hat, as she wrote. Feeling that she was on trial, Virginia outlined the sermon she would deliver: fifteen minutes on the four questions Jesus will ask at the Judgment; fifteen minutes on salvation and forgiveness; and fifteen minutes on Jesus's last hour on the cross and the three who were with him at its foot—Mary, his mother; Mary of Magdala; and John, who represent love, forgiveness, and service. Finally, she asserted that she would follow prayers written by the Apostles "long before the so-called Christians in their zeal and stupidity frustrated the purposes of the Almighty by fragmentation and denominational talk." The framework for the first half hour of the sermon corresponds to what she preached on Good Friday to the Episcopalians at Calvary Church, as published in *Credos & Quips*. However, for the attendees at the Salvation Army or Goodwill Chapels, she would have chosen different examples from daily life to illustrate the questions. They would not have had extra clothing to give away.

The Goodwill Chapel invited Virginia to deliver a sermon to the Jews who came there on Monday in the Christian Holy Week. The chapel representative was confident that she would not treat the Jews as outsiders. My grandmother did not explain any further, but we know that many years earlier, she had welcomed enthusiastically the two Jews who came to her 1922 Sunday school class in Cloverport. She wrote that they were "deprived by distance of their synagogue."

The fifty or so Christians "learned a great deal" from the two Jews, Virginia observed. Always practical and with an eye on the eternal, she remarked, "If one day we are to sit with Abraham, Isaac, and Jacob in the Kingdom of Heaven, we'd do well to get into practice now." She concluded that "if you study the history of the Jewish people without the assistance of Jews, you never really know it" (*Close Your Eyes*, 14).

My grandmother summarized the Goodwill Chapel sermon for my mother in a letter that opens with a remark on Queen Mary's death, which dates the letter on or after March 24, 1953, a Tuesday. Holy Week began on March 30 in 1953, and Easter fell on April 5, so the sermon probably occurred on March 30 of that year. Virginia expressed the gratitude owed to the Hebrew people for the Bible and the knowledge of the one true God, and she underscored the Jewish heritage of Jesus and his mother. "The founders of Christianity were all Jews," she asserted. Furthermore, the "Jews had carried the torch of faith down through the ages through pestilence, famine, world deluge, slavery, and bondage." Virginia's conclusion brought tears to some eyes when she said, "No religion deserves the scorn of another and those who scorn represent the antichrist because scorn has no place in Christ's teachings." The men who filed out shook her hand and told her they were glad they had come. Outside the chapel, a man pressed a mezuzah into her hand. Virginia gave it a special place at home and instructed my mother to be sure she was buried with it in one hand, a rosary in the other, and a cross on her heart (*Flapdoodle*, 76).

Clearing Debris on the Highway to Glory

Virginia's lively teaching on biblical women in *Close Your Eyes When Praying* exudes empathy and down-to-earth common sense as well as a taste for adventure in reading. As my mother explained in "Ah, Dear Readers,"

> Mother loved the Bible—people and words. To
> her very considerable knowledge of the Bible, she

contributed a remarkably winsome and amusing enchanting charm, a capacity for retelling the great Bible stories in terms of the daily life she knew in Kentucky and the larger world through which she wandered as occasion might permit. She spoke as naturally and as casually about biblical personalities as she would about her neighbors and acquaintances. She was, let us say, on speaking terms with many of them. Her affection for all kinds of people was reflected in the fascination with which she clung to the stories of biblical personalities. Mother's Bible was a book of people, and she was forever detecting something worthwhile in the biblical rogues and some blemishment in the biblical heroes. Mother was blessed with a knack for storytelling ... She entranced people with her prancing recollections and her contagious humor. She was especially delighted to recall her own follies and foibles.

My grandmother pictures Eve, alone in a garden with a stranger, with no mother to advise her, and with the devil whispering in her ear (*Close Your Eyes*, 36). As one who lost her firstborn child, a son, Virginia empathizes with both Eve and Bathsheba. Tradition recorded David's lament for Absalom; my grandmother makes her listeners aware that Bathsheba must have endured great sorrow (*Close Your Eyes*, 54). My grandmother's interest in Judith led her to tiptoe into the pulpit and check the rector's Bible to see if his version included the Apocrypha, which it did, while the Bibles provided for her class did not (*Close Your Eyes*, 87). Virginia had no use for the biblical commentators she consulted, particularly when it came to the role of Eve.

Poor Eve has been the clay-pigeon toward which all the pigeon-hearted theologians and estimable Bible commentators have taken aim with their popguns. As a result countless generations of otherwise relatively sane human beings have been bamboozled into believing that the daughters of Eve are the root of all evil. (*Close Your Eyes*, 30)

My grandmother's reading of the story of Adam and Eve boldly rejects the authority of established "bewhiskered" commentators and proceeds according to two techniques that feminist critics and readers would later advocate: "reader response criticism," the subjective reaction to reading a text, and the practice of telling the story from the perspective of the person in the story whose voice was silenced.[150] Virginia explains her first approach: "So let's leave the bewhiskered Bible commentators in their stuffy towers! Instead of their bloodless exposés about Eve—may she rest in peace—let us consider her as only women can. What I shall read here is according to my own instinctive feelings" (*Close Your Eyes*, 24). As for the second technique, Virginia gives Eve a voice to express her sorrow at the death of Abel.

Between the lines of Holy Scripture I would like to add these words: "And when he that was first dead upon the earth was covered by the earth, the mother of all living cried unto God, saying, 'Oh, give me back my boy.' But neither God nor her reason answered her, and looking about she girded herself to live ... The tears Eve shed over the body of Abel never ceased." (*Close Your Eyes*, 35)

Virginia's comments throughout her lesson imagine what Eve might have felt. Adam, from my grandmother's point of view, did only two important things: "'he ate' and 'he begat.'" "How many of his descendants to this very day," she exclaims, "seem chiefly to be interested in only these two pastimes!" (*Close Your Eyes*, 32).

Reviews of *Close Your Eyes When Praying* reveal that my grandmother's reading of the Bible from a woman's perspective held considerable interest for women reviewers and readers. Anne B. Boardman, book editor for *Foundations for Christian Living*, placed

Close Your Eyes When Praying on her list of books recommended for Christmas 1968. "In a delightfully engaging book Mrs. Hudson interprets the feelings, hopes and aspirations of the women in the Bible," Boardman wrote. "To her they are real people whom she knows and understands. Some have faults but she points out those who come through with flying colors. Easy and rewarding reading."[151] Eugenia Price, in a review for which I have no place of publication or date, made a pressing case for the book: "I urge everyone to read *Close Your Eyes When Praying!* There can't be too many of these 'pure delight' volumes from the yellowing notes of Virginia Cary Hudson." She concluded, "Virginia Cary Hudson scribbled her provocative lines a long time ago—but we need them today."

Early in 1969, Constance Page Daniel, in "A Little Gem of a Book," concluded that the "book is a must for any churchwoman who admits to being over twenty-five." She described the book as "a slightly irreverent interpretation ('Bathsheba gave up her ambition to become Miss Israel of 1000 B.C.')" but "witty, wise and often poignant in its message, from the compassionate defense of Eve to the quiet majesty of Mary." Daniel chose one of my grandmother's sayings to summarize her teaching: "If you remember nothing else that I have said in class, try to remember this. After life is over and done, there is absolutely nothing worth a darn except kindness" (*Close Your Eyes,* 67–68).[152]

H. F. Davidson, in the *Presbyterian Record*, described *Close Your Eyes When Praying* as "a collection of whimsical insightful studies on women of the Bible." Davidson concluded that the "studies reveal more about the teacher than about the Bible characters she deals with, although she does make each one come to life. There are several hints that Bible commentators, being mere males, have failed to understand the women of the Bible."[153] A review by *Eternity Book Service* observed that "most of the men in the Bible tried to avoid God's call or talk their way out of it," while Virginia asked, "Where in the Bible do you find a woman responding to God's call with equivocations, rationalizations, or alibis?" (*Close Your Eyes,* 103).[154]

My grandmother's perspective on the Bible gained a review from the Roman Catholic press that included her essays with articles that approached scripture from the growing feminist perspective. The author viewed favorably Virginia's defense of women, namely Eve, Elizabeth, and Mary, against biblical men and male biblical commentators.

On Eve, Virginia declares, "I think we can understand her, but I very much doubt if any man ever could." She goes on to say, "One Bible commentator writes, 'At best, Eve is an enigma.' Imagine! What, I wonder, does he think that Eve is at worst?" (*Close Your Eyes*, 24). With regard to Adam, she observes that he shows Eve no affection.

> Those of us who are romantically inclined would like to read here that Adam loved Eve. There is, however, not even the inference that Adam was even pleased with her or that he looked favorably upon her. In other words, Adam presumably said, "Get going, my little helpmate, and see what you can do to make yourself useful." A man could read these verses without any qualms, but not a woman. (*Close Your Eyes*, 28)

Virginia, again as a woman reader, points out that both Elizabeth and Mary stand out for their trust and readiness to believe God's word. Elizabeth was ready to believe the angel's message about her pregnancy, while Zachariah was not. The Roman Catholic press reviewer observed that Virginia "concluded that women perhaps have a greater ability to believe, possibly because 'women are themselves creators of miracles. After having given birth to a child, nothing else seems beyond belief'" (*Close Your Eyes*, 114).

My grandmother takes her interpretation of the Visitation, Mary's journey to speak with Elizabeth, a step further. First she underscores Elizabeth's parallel role in the biblical narrative. "But the story of Mary, beautiful in detail and language, is a pie crust without shortening if we fail to include the parallel story of Mary's kinswoman, Elizabeth" (*Close Your Eyes*, 111). Where scripture remains silent about the two women's conversation, Virginia summarizes the topics they would have discussed and creates a dialogue in which they might have engaged (*Close Your Eyes*, 115–16).

The reviewer mentioned that one of my grandmother's class members resigned after a class on Mary and objected, "We Protestants don't believe in Mary" (*Close Your Eyes*, 108). The reviewer applauded Virginia as "a woman who would have been an ecumenical leader were she alive today." Virginia "blamed 'esteemed theologians' and 'estimable churchmen' for creating the arguments and confusions surrounding 'the simple role which God gave to this guileless young woman to play in His cosmic plan of redemption ... So perhaps it is up to us (women) to cut through the theological fat and find the true picture'" (*Close Your Eyes*, 98).

Finally, the reviewer cited the following sentence of Virginia's: "I can't stand women preachers, but I wonder if something wonderful might happen if the women were to take over the church" (*Close Your Eyes*, 114). Which half of the sentence did the reviewer want to emphasize? I wish I could ask my grandmother, who preached at two chapels in Louisville and called herself a preacher, why she said this about women preachers. She herself was criticized for teaching her Sunday class. The woman who objected to my grandmother's discussion of Mary added that she "intended to seek out some sanctuary where God's Word was undefiled by the words of a woman" (*Close Your Eyes*, 109). My grandmother's advocacy for the study of women in the Bible from a woman's perspective ruffled some feathers. A woman teaching in an Episcopal church about biblical women and about Christian belief was forging new territory in the late 1940s and early 1950s. A woman preaching to diverse audiences in a nondenominational chapel stood even further ahead of her time.

What can we say about Virginia's beliefs and approach to faith? She makes it clear in *Credos & Quips* and *Close Your Eyes When Praying* that she accepts the teachings of the church and the Bible, as specified in the three Christian creeds. When discussing Mary, she defends the virgin birth, "because it is clearly a Biblical teaching and it is clearly a teaching of the Church." For the creed she asserts that "twenty centuries of believers have tested and tried, believed and experienced, the matters contained in the Creed. Somewhere along the way someone would have conclusively proved an error if there were an error" (*Close Your Eyes*, 105).

Yet my grandmother did not judge people of other beliefs and creeds. Aware that she was not traditional in this respect, she described to her class three "circles of loyalties" (*Close Your Eyes*, 109).

> I hope you won't think of me as a heretic if I say that the loyalties my heart cherishes are like concentric circles. The largest circle encloses all of God's children everywhere. I am not concerned if they are big or little, rich or poor, kings or peasants. My spiritual spectacles do not show me their skin color. My hearing makes no distinction between mumbo-jumbo and eloquent syntax. That they are human beings, fashioned in the image of the Almighty, makes them my brothers and sisters. God loves them, and I try to do likewise. (*Close Your Eyes*, 109)

In the second circle are all Christians, and the third encloses Episcopalians. However, her love for her own church does not imply that she loves others less. On the contrary, she says, "Perhaps for this reason I love others more. I hope so" (*Close Your Eyes*, 110). My grandmother describes her work as "one woman's campaign to clear up the debris that clutters the highway to Glory" (*Close Your Eyes*, 110).

Virginia's individual approach to faith emerges from her writings. She emphasizes the need for prayer and the hope that springs from it. She frequently rephrases scriptural passages, such as the favorite Matthew 7:7, "Knock and it shall be opened unto you." She teaches, "Knock and the door of faith will be opened unto you," and then she steps back to emphasize, "But you have got to knock" (*Close Your Eyes*, 63). Elsewhere she bypasses the knock and goes straight for the door handle: "Take a firm grip on the handle of prayer, and open the door."[155]

For Virginia, day-to-day hope rises not only from prayer but from a belief in the unexpected and miraculous, as transmitted in the intervention of angels. Angels and their wings float across many of my grandmother's writings, beginning with *O Ye Jigs & Juleps!* and ending in her letters to me, her granddaughter. In *O Ye Jigs & Juleps!* young Virginia declares, "Everybody grows wings in Heaven, and then I can fly, and that will be wonderful." She muses that she could use her wings to fly to Paris, if they don't molt, like her canary's feathers. "I sure will need all of my feathers to get across the ocean and back again to Heaven" (*Jigs & Juleps*, 24).

In her late fifties, Virginia tackles the question of angels head-on. The immediate subject in *Close Your Eyes* is the angel's appearance to Mary, a prickly topic for those Episcopalians who lean strongly toward simple Protestant beliefs and fiercely away from anything that seems "popish." My grandmother posits the objections that come from her listeners: "No angel ever spoke to me"; "I never saw an angel or touched his hand"; "Only children believe in angels"; and "Angels are part of the fanciful poetry of religion, and we are not supposed to believe in them literally." She defends her belief in angels with a powerful statement of the ways that God has touched her life.

> But angels have nudged my arm when I've stood at the kitchen sink. Angels have pointed the way when I have been lost in an endless labyrinth. Angels have placed my head on their shoulders when I have been despondent and blue. Angels have cheered me when I have nursed a broken heart. Angels have wiped my eyes when the death of a loved one has made me want to die.

"God's messages and messengers are all about us," she asserts. Paraphrasing the gospel, she continues, "But you have got to have eyes that see and you've got to have ears that hear." Her following words, "Eyes for the invisible and ears for the inaudible," echo the ancient Christian notion of spiritual sight and hearing (*Close Your Eyes*, 103).

Her belief in heavenly life combines with the intervention of angels in earthly life. The young Virginia devoted an essay to "Everlasting Life," observing that, "When you go to heaven with your Everlasting Life that makes you an angel, and Peter, or Moses, or somebody, lines you all up and passes out the crown and the harps" (*Jigs & Juleps*, 24). Virginia the adult teacher and preacher defended the life everlasting affirmed in the creed. Virginia as my grandmother instilled belief in heaven through the letters and drawings she did for me, her four-year-old granddaughter.

This message of hope does not deny another teaching of the creed, the Last Judgment. As she declares in *Credos & Quips*, "This place of everlasting damnation is becoming more and more unpopular with some people ... They just love to hear about Heaven, but when you talk about Hell, they want you to hurry up, and shut up" (*Credos*, 44). The four questions from her Good Friday sermon constitute the criteria for Judgment. They all concern our treatment of other human beings. Virginia sums this up for her Sunday class with imagery from horse racing: "When the course of our lives is run and we cross the finish line, if we have, in our running, bumped and hindered those alongside of us and made their going harder, although we may win, the victory will be ashes on our tongues" (*Close Your Eyes*, 68).

My grandmother espoused traditional beliefs with an emphasis on prayer, on the divine presence in everyday occurrences, and on belief in life everlasting. All three elements provided hope during hardship and fueled determination to make the best of every moment. She underscored the need to be tolerant and understanding of others, to put ourselves in their shoes, whether they be living human beings of any sort or scriptural characters. Some of the episodes in *Flapdoodle, Trust & Obey* illustrate how my grandmother intervened as a hopeful presence in the lives of people she knew and met, sensing what they needed and finding a way to provide it.

Flapdoodle, Trust & Obey

My grandmother wrote stories about her everyday life and the doings of her family, the people who worked for her, her neighbors, roomers, visitors, and characters who came to the door; updates on the neighborhood of St. James Court and her role as president of the St. James Court Association; accounts of people and events at the church; reflections on world events and how they affected local people—the local boys who died in World War II or who were sent to Korea at the beginning of the war there, the soldiers who survived and came back to thank her for the hospitality she had offered when they had returned to Louisville on leave, her suspicions that the fighting would escalate; and so on. All these she incorporated into letters to my mother. A colorful microcosm centered on her home and the people of 1453 St. James Court reached outward to embrace a sphere of people and events that belonged to a transitional decade in American and world history.

Familiar themes from my grandmother's other writings run through the letters in *Flapdoodle*. Virginia joined reflections on eternal life with the thought of flying on angel's wings. She mourned the loss of a friend and asked God to watch over her in heaven. She imagined herself flying above her friend's earthly dwelling and looking down.

> When I fly over Mrs. Amesbury's mansion, I will be glad that I don't have to hunt all over heaven for help to clean up the place. I'll fly back to my little house with one window, pull my rocking chair out onto a cloud, and eat crabmeat and drink Coca-Cola. Every afternoon I'll go down to the Pearly Gates and try my best to persuade old Saint Peter to let in every woman who had to work for a living. (*Flapdoodle*, 20)

Virginia humorously envisioned herself as an advocate for women, even in the afterlife. Fittingly, some advertisements for *Flapdoodle* featured angels.

Virginia's friend's death brought to mind the loss of her firstborn son, and she grieved for him, just as she did when speaking about the biblical mothers Eve and Bathsheba. When Mrs. Amesbury lay on her deathbed in an asylum, my grandmother pleaded with God to come for her, to send his angel or her own son. "Send my own child, Lord. You came and took him from me. Tell him his mother asks him to take poor Mrs. Amesbury across the Jordan. And when my own time comes, Lord, please send my own child after me so I won't be afraid and lonesome"(*Flapdoodle*, 19). Virginia employed biblical imagery, the Jordan, and biblical characters, in this case Gabriel, to convey her feelings on the passing of people from this world.

Virginia issued warnings to her daughter about the church and its politics. She boiled down the organizational descriptions of church groups into straight talk after her election to chair a committee:

> In Kentucky the Auxiliary contains the bosses and the Guild contains the workers in the churches. The Auxiliary members are the blabbers and popper-offers. The Guild attends the altar, looks after the church supplies, and sews for the hospital, orphanage, and home for unmarried mothers. The Auxiliary uses your brains, and the Guild uses your hands. Ask your minister how his church women are organized, and then get into the group that most appeals to you. (*Flapdoodle*, 17–18)

My mother used her hands and her brains for the church. She served on the altar guild, managed the white elephant table every year for the church bazaar, organized many social events, entertained substitute clergy, and more. She also gave talks about the church to the Women's Auxiliary, as my grandmother did.

My grandmother advised my mother on other topics, such as the perils of living in the country (*Flapdoodle*, 11–13): "But don't build your nest away out in the bushes where a milkman will need a road map to find you and from where you'll have to wade in mud to get a bus." She told the story of a Louisville woman who worked for her and did her laundry to the tune of the Scottish march "The Campbells Are Coming." The woman and husband moved to a farm where the old saying "If the creek don't rise" did not ward off misfortune. The creek did rise, and disaster flooded in (*Flapdoodle*, 11). The woman returned to the city and told my grandmother the story during a chance meeting. My mother heeded my grandmother's warning about country living. She never lived more than a mile from a grocery store. My own family's apartment lies within five minutes' walk of two food stores! Other lessons from my grandmother to my mother included the six ages of womanhood (*Flapdoodle*, 23–25), the rules bride and groom should follow for a happy marriage (*Flapdoodle*, 83–85), and the joys of grandmotherhood (*Flapdoodle,* 87–91).

Virginia found adventure in a variety of places. At the fair, she "wandered along, expecting something to happen. It always does" (*Flapdoodle*, 39). One of the happenings involved a partially sighted old woman and a hungry little boy. They had been allowed to ask for alms from the crowd at the fair. My grandmother first took the boy and bought him milk and a sandwich. Then she instructed the woman to sing loudly, "Gabriel, I'm out on a limb ..." Virginia had the woman sit on her folding chair while she stood next to her, ringing a bell as forcefully as she could and calling out, "Keep your dime, Brother, and put in a quarter." A sightseeing bus passed by, and a hand stretched out to give my grandmother a dollar. She replied with the Bible in mind, specifically the parable of Lazarus and Dives, the rich man (Luke 16:19–31). "Thanks for the crumbs from Dives' table," she quipped. In a moment she realized that she was looking into the eyes of her diocesan bishop. To his "Why, Virginia, what on earth are you doing?" she replied, "Just trying to practice what you preach, Right Reverend" (*Flapdoodle*, 44). Virginia livened up even the most austere surroundings, namely the courtroom, when she defended herself in one case concerning a car accident and let the judge have a piece of her mind in another when she served as a juror (*Flapdoodle*, 35–38). As she closed one letter, "Heavens! Whoever said that life is dull?" (*Flapdoodle*, 44).

In another letter she recounted a tale of cruelty that set in motion generations of revenge. A slave's death from a beating resulted in a spell that was cast upon a chest of drawers, ca. 1830, formerly passed from one generation to the next in my family and now the property of the Kentucky Historical Society (*Flapdoodle*, 45–53). One of my grandmother's female ancestors married a wealthy man whose father was "the devil incarnate," according to my grandmother and her grandmother before her. While the young bride of one of the evil man's sons awaited the birth of a child, a slave made the child a magnificent chest. Finding fault with the chest, the evil father beat the slave until he died. The other slaves put a curse of revenge on the chest, sprinkling dried owl's blood in the drawers and chanting a dirge of conjure. The new baby was the chest's first victim. The chest passed from one household to another for several generations. After fifteen more victims, my grandmother began to wonder, "Were these mere coincidences and nothing more?" and she asked Sallie (Annie in *Flapdoodle*) if she knew how to break a conjure. Sallie explained how the ritual would work, but the first step depended on chance, a dead owl brought by a good friend. After several days of carrying out the ritual, Sallie revealed that if the curse were removed successfully, Sallie or my grandmother would die. To my grandmother's heartbreak, Sallie was gone in a few months at the age of sixty-nine.

Among *Flapdoodle*'s stories, the tale of the chest and the sorrow surrounding it probably haunts the soul more than any other. For years, the chest stood in an unoccupied room in my parents' house, with the knobs either turned inward or removed so that no one could put anything in the drawers by accident. Before my mother gave the chest to the Kentucky Historical Society, she asked if I wanted it, but I refused it, as I had several years earlier when my husband and I married. It was not that my mother urged me to have the chest. She wanted to ensure that it was preserved. Moreover, she always made clear that I could have any of the family furniture I desired to keep. However, I wanted no part of the chest's disturbing history, from the cruel killing of the man who made the chest to Sallie's death to break the spell.

My mother sought a safe place for the chest in order to preserve its history and to prevent a future owner from its spell. Evidence for the chest's power was overwhelming. Moreover, the practice of conjuration seems to have been widespread. The ritual of conjuration that my grandmother described corresponds to that found in slave narratives such as that of Henry Bibb of Kentucky. The rituals involved the sprinkling of powders and the chanting of formulas designed to cast spells against cruel slave owners.[156] But how much evidence remains for the effective breaking of spells? Could Sallie's death truly have expunged so potent a conjure? My mother did not want to take risks with anyone's life.

The letter about the chest occupies three single-spaced pages. Other letters vary from a few lines to a few paragraphs. Sometimes my grandmother wrote more than one letter to my mother in the same day. If she had written a letter saying that she did not feel well, she would send a telegram to arrive before the letter and reassure my mother that she was better before my mother could get upset by the letter. Kidney stones shifted and ground together in unpredictable, painful, and dangerous ways. The tone of my grandmother's letters varied according to the day, the moment, and even the movement of the stones. My grandmother's drawings of herself showed different expressions, whether tears, a smile, or a frown.

My mother was not exempted from my grandmother's stern advice. One letter warns Mother about her stubborn tenacity and begins, "My little turtle." The letter centers around the behavior of a snapping turtle, analogous to my mother's dogged refusal to let go of ideas or plans. Still the letter's tone conveys love, concern, and a sense of humor. The snapping turtle–like tenacity surely helped my mother persevere in the quest to publish my grandmother's writings.

Questions about the genuineness of the letters arose in a review by Madelon Golden, "An Old-Fashioned Spring Tonic" (*Post Dispatch*, St. Louis, MO, April 3, 1966). A response to Golden and the questions she raised merits a detour here. Golden first described *Flapdoodle* as "Another small gem full of sense and nonsense," but then she remarked on *Flapdoodle* and *O Ye Jigs & Juleps!*:

But, close scrutiny is not invited, except for those charming illustrations by Richard Rosenblum or the skillful editing of Charles L. Wallis. (Did he help create the sassy style of our old-fashioned girl? Was there really a Virginia, Santa Claus?) As a book, it's a spoonful of spring tonic. Flapdoodle, trust and obey![157]

Golden seems to imply that the editor created my grandmother's style and, furthermore, that someone else's voice hid behind the charm of the child Virginia. Neither insinuation is accurate. Whether the editing and combining of multiple letters results in a "sassy" tone, I cannot say, but the voice throughout the narrative is that of my grandmother, who was consistently spirited, quick-witted, and often humorous.

Golden also criticized my grandmother's "Old South philosophy":

Some readers who look beyond the laughs may wonder whether Little Mama's Old South philosophy is as timely as her prose. As one of the good-hearted "white folks" she is oh-so-appreciative of Negroes as servants. For example, she buries Sister Annie, a devoted family toiler for 58 years, in a wooden box in a cinder-gravel packed grave midst a cornfield, after a "collection for the family." Sister Annie apparently earned little else than highest praise from Little Mama, who believes in "the intelligence of white blood, the faithfulness of black blood, and the mannerisms of blue blood."

Golden undoubtedly objected to the racial and social attitudes behind the words she quoted. By 1966, the civil rights movement had achieved the passing of landmark legislation, the Civil Rights Act of 1964 and the Voting Rights Act of 1965. Sensitivity to racist language had grown in many quarters even while prejudice remained. Racial prejudice across the South and in the North continued to show its horrific, violent effects, and the entire country could see it on television. Martin Luther King Jr. was focusing attention on the de facto segregation of northern cities, particularly Chicago.[158]

However, the phrase that joins attributes to blood color does not provide sufficient grounds to characterize my grandmother as a stereotypical southerner, particularly not as one who did not care for or about the people who worked for her. The objectionable words do not in fact describe Annie. They appear in the story of the conjured chest and describe Aunty Cherry, "as good a woman as the Lord ever made," who was hired as a nurse for my great-grandmother (*Flapdoodle*, 49). Moreover, Golden removes the passage about Annie's burial from significant elements of the context. My grandmother drove six of Annie's friends to the undertaker's parlor, where my grandmother was the only white person in attendance. The community took up a collection for the family, and Annie's family buried her in the accustomed manner and place (*Flapdoodle*, 30–34). Missing from the published letter is the description of the cornfield, "the plowed ground they call a cemetery."

About Annie, whose real name was Sallie, my grandmother observed, "Annie was the most ladylike, the kindest, most patient and unselfish person, black or white, I ever knew" (*Flapdoodle*, 30). In Sallie's memory, my grandmother closed the dining room for a while and hung Annie's cane in the kitchen, "hoping that its sanctifying presence may instill in all who look upon it some small portion of the great qualities she possessed. Trust and obey" (*Flapdoodle*, 34). Throughout the letters in *Flapdoodle* and the other correspondence I have in my possession, the deep affection my grandmother felt for Sallie and other household workers speaks strongly, along with their trust in her and her responsibility for them all their lives.

Certainly my grandmother grew up in a southern social structure. "Sister Annie" (Sallie) helped to raise my mother and my aunt. Sallie's older sister worked for my great-grandmother, and their mother, "Aunt Margaret," worked for my great-grandmother's mother. In contrast to my grandmother, some residents of St. James Court and vicinity would hire only white household workers. From time to time, my grandmother wrote about neighbors who hired only whites, and she complained about the people who called her when they needed short-term hired help for a specific task. Refusing to deal directly with blacks, they asked her to find laborers for them. She was irritated at her neighbors' distrust and their lack of what she saw as a responsibility to find and create regular work for people who needed jobs. Once she wrote to my mother angrily about a neighbor who refused any financial help to someone who had worked for him for twenty years. My grandmother stepped in, wrote a "note" for him, and hired him to do jobs around St. James Court in order to pay it back.

My grandmother had electric wiring put in a household worker's house, so that the woman, Carrie, would not ignite a fire with the lantern she was using for light. Carrie also reported that my grandmother called the hospital and sent Frank directly there when he was "moaning and cramping" and "couldn't make his water."[159] When Carrie's knee was injured, my grandmother took her straight to the hospital, where the staff ignored her despite her inability to stand. Furious that the hospital would not provide a wheelchair for Carrie, my grandmother went outside and recruited a policeman to come to the hospital desk and insist that Carrie be given a wheelchair.[160] My grandmother's letters refer to Sallie many times. Sallie filled the house with her songs and stories. She came to work for my grandmother even when she felt the weight of having been hired out for work at the age of eleven. When Sallie was tired, she and my grandmother divided up the housework. When she was sick, my grandmother put her to bed for the day, brought her meals, drove her home when needed, and had her sleep at the house, where my grandmother kept a room available for her. Within the *Flapdoodle* letters, my grandmother wrote of her grief almost two years after Sallie's death: "Annie has been gone twenty months yesterday ... The place she has left in my heart could not be filled by the moon and all the stars ... I was not prepared for the Gethsemane of her passing" (*Flapdoodle*, 77).[161]

William, whom my grandmother described with great affection

in her adult letters, stayed with or near the family for much of his life. She also mentioned him in the essays that were published in *O Ye Jigs & Juleps!* He taught her dances while she waited on the train platform for her father to arrive, and she wanted to whitewash him so that he could come to school with her. She recalled as an adult that William, whose name was changed to Washington in *Flapdoodle*, "took me to school, taught me to curry a horse, to brush out its tail, to adjust a martingale, to judge the length of a check rein and the snugness of a saddle girth, to handle both reins with one hand." But the life skills William taught young Virginia were not limited to horsemanship; he also instructed her on how "to pick a chicken and bathe a dog." William helped her get her clothes out of the house when she eloped at age sixteen, and his were the "sympathetic arms into which [she] sank, overcome with indignant wrath and youthful heartbreak after [her] humiliating arrest and forcible return." Forty years after William gave her an important lesson in self-defense, to "aim true for a weak spot and then swing with all your might," she managed to chase a burglar from the house. William worked for the family for thirty-five years and then for the railroad. He had no insurance and told his boss that he was not worried, because "Little Miss would come and get him." Alerted to his death, my grandmother found his body in an undertaker's warehouse, about to be taken to the potter's field, more commonly called the "boneyard," as she wrote in a December 30, 1946, letter. William had served in World War I, and Virginia sent a wire to Washington, DC, to secure funeral costs and a burial spot for him in the Zachary Taylor National Cemetery in Louisville.[162] She also ensured that his sister would receive the railroad retirement funds that he had put aside each month. It had been nearly ten years since R. N. Hudson's death, and some of the employees who greeted and thanked Virginia must have remembered her.

Yes, Sallie, Emma, William, Carrie, and others worked for my grandmother and her family, and she relied on them, but she also cared about and for them. They relied on my grandmother too, until the end, when they knew that "Miss Virginia" would make sure that they received a decent burial.

All her life, Virginia created communities of celebration for the people she knew and met; she valued people's distinctive gifts, sensed their needs, and spread joy for life. As a young girl she organized a garden party with her beloved neighbor Mrs. Harris and invited everyone she knew, including the children at the orphanage, "the little colored boys down on the station platform," and the bishop. After a Corinthian julep, the bishop played Skip to my Lou and danced with Mrs. Harris while Virginia played hymns in ragtime. The orphans danced the Virginia reel. Virginia encouraged the African American boys to join her in dancing to ragtime, the buck-and-wing, go down Moses, and kitten on the keys, dances they had taught her while she waited each day for her father to arrive at the train station.[163]

Religion and the Bible were always woven tightly into Virginia's living and thinking. As a girl she defended her practices and beliefs fiercely. When her mother obliged her to attend the Campbellites' church party, she wore her hat, which prompted a Campbellite girl to laugh at her. The sometimes pejorative term *Campbellite* generally refers to Christians who trace their roots to the nineteenth-century American Restoration Movement. An argument ensued between the two girls over St. Paul's instruction on wearing hats or not wearing hats. When the Campbellite girl insulted St. Paul by saying "Fooie" on him, Virginia retaliated by slapping and pinching her. Virginia's mother disciplined her daughter by requiring a quiet hour of reading St. Paul (*Jigs and Juleps*, 41–42). As an adult Virginia continued to defend and propagate her faith with strength, but that faith grew in open-mindedness toward the beliefs of others. She practiced religious tolerance and advocated it through her teaching and preaching in her own church and in nondenominational chapels.

A woman of strong faith, Virginia loved her church but recognized and criticized its shortcomings, notably its neglect of women's views. She cherished the opportunity to speak to women about women in her Sunday class at Calvary Episcopal Church in

Louisville, Kentucky. Virginia presented her Sunday class as a time for women to be themselves and not tend to family members' needs: "The next thirty minutes represent a reprieve from all of this. At this time we can be women in our rights, talk like women, think like women, and glory in our womanliness" (*Close Your Eyes*, 49).

Virginia, who loved and paraphrased hymns, offered a woman's parody of "O Day of Rest and Gladness," known in the Episcopal hymnal as a "Hymn for the Lord's Day" (*The Hymnal 1940*, 474). "What is the Lord's Day for womenfolk?" she asked.

> O day of noise and commotion—when the children are home from school!
>
> O day of rushing and serving—when hubby, freed from the toils of the workaday world, lounges and loafs and clutters.
>
> O day of cooking and dishwashing—when everyone wants fried chicken for dinner, ham for supper, and "something to fill us up" before bedtime.
>
> O day of gobble and gobbledegook—when distant friends, long-lost relatives, and nonkissing cousins drop by "for just a moment"—providentially just at eating time—and leave long after the sidewalks have been rolled up for the night. (*Close Your Eyes*, 49)

For women who work at home, Virginia asserted, Monday represented not a "blue" day but a chance for rest after the many obligations of Sunday. Parish clergy, I may add, see Monday in a similar way, and so would their spouses, if they had the good fortune of not working on Monday. When I was a rector's wife, I found Sundays totally exhausting, and Mondays provided little respite. My husband rarely had a day of rest, no matter the day of the week.

Virginia sustained herself on life's journey with hopeful belief and with prayer, whether spontaneous, on-the-spot "Come down, Lord, come down"; historical prayers that she discovered in research; or poetic prayers that she composed, such as this one that I found tucked in my scrapbook.

Lest you forget the lasting thing,
I give you when we part,
A prayer for your safe keeping,
Locked fast within my heart.
May God in His own mercy,
Protect you in His way:
May He bless you in the darkness,
And guide you thru each day.

Prayers spring from Virginia's writing. She often repeated her favorite sayings: "Trust and Obey," "Say your prayers and keep trying," "Take a firm grip on the handle of prayer, and open the door." Virginia prayed in the midst of letters, and in her talks she prayed on behalf of biblical women.

Virginia's biblical usage often reflected the words and liturgy of the Book of Common Prayer (1928) and the *Hymnal 1940. How, some wondered, would she know by heart the* Benedicite, omnia opera Domini *(Bless all the works of the Lord)? Or any of the Psalms? A ten-year-old does not use language like that!* The questions have a ready answer and the challenge a quick rebuttal. Open the 1928 Book of Common Prayer! Virginia and her congregation sang the Benedicite in English at morning prayer, with its many lines beginning "O Ye ..." The text is found with its Latin title Benedicite, omnia opera Domini in the Book of Common Prayer (11–13) and with music in the *Hymnal 1940* (612). To an editor's question, "Wasn't the Latin too 'highfollutin' to use?" my mother replied that it was part of Episcopal worship. She sent the publisher an Episcopal Book Club bookmark that reproduced the first verse in English and the title in Latin. I found a dozen or more of these in my mother's files. Surely she handed the bookmarks to people who doubted that her mother as a child would know such phrases.

I still remember well the canticles of morning prayer—the music and the words—and in the background I can hear my father next to me, booming them out in his bass voice. When I sang in the church choir during the last years of elementary school, my father helped me learn how to sing the canticles for morning prayer, particularly the Venite, exultemus Domino; the Benedicite, and the Jubilate Deo, which is taken from Psalm 100. The children's choir frequently practiced these and the other canticles from morning prayer, and we always referred to them by their Latin names.

A faithful churchgoer, my grandmother took many responsibilities as a lay leader. She loved to learn and to teach, and she did not shy from preaching. Moreover, faith in God took priority over membership in the Episcopal Church, and she radiated the essentials of that faith in one God to audiences that included various Protestants, Jews, a Mormon bishop, and members of the House of David. She confided to her daughter that she still had difficulty with stuttering when called upon to speak without notes in a formal setting. She did not hesitate to accept speaking and preaching invitations, but she provided herself with copious notes, the core of the religious essays we still have.

Fun-loving, strong-minded, mischievous, and imaginative as a child, Virginia preserved those qualities in adulthood. Carrie, who knew Virginia all her life, observed that "Pretty [Virginia]," when she was ten years old, was "one bad child" and that "she's not changed a bit, except she's got higher and wider" (*Flapdoodle*, 96). Virginia herself asserted, "I have been able to retain through the years a modicum of childlikeness" (*Close Your Eyes,* 67). She entered readily into the world of children and enjoyed grandmotherhood immensely. At her death she had two granddaughters, whom she loved dearly, myself and my cousin. Living far from her, I received letters that connected us in spirit when we were apart.

Chapter 4

"Ah, Dear Readers"

My mother dreamed of imparting to other readers my grandmother's lively character, humor, and imagination. My grandmother had expressed the desire to publish some of her writings, but she never initiated a process. She kept writing, traveling, observing, teaching, preaching, and writing it all down. After my grandmother's death in 1954, my mother slowly worked through her grief by assembling all her mother's writings and typing out the handwritten originals that remained. She began to send her mother's childhood essays to presses in 1958. After each of the seventeen rejections and more, she moved from discouragement to greater resolve. She negotiated the price for publishing with a vanity press over several months, but the cost proved prohibitive. My mother did not give up. She was uplifted by sheer determination, by love, and by prayer. In the words learned from my grandmother, she often said, "Say your prayers and keep trying." In moments of disappointment, she also uttered a favorite saying of her mother's, "Trust and obey," the title of an old hymn. My mother succeeded in making her mother's writings known in four books published with leading presses!

My mother also started to write her own account of her mother's life and writings, especially the story of publishing *O Ye Jigs & Juleps!* For years, she gathered materials, jotted down notes, and talked of her dream to write a book she would entitle "Ah,

Dear Readers." In a letter to one of her editors who had encouraged her, my mother wrote, "Should 'Ah, dear readers' never, ever be written, or if written become the pages of a book, I will always keep your letter expressing the hope that I will try to write. It tickles me clear down to my toes. Trust and Obey, Virginia." The refrain of the hymn "Trust and Obey" goes, "Trust and obey for there's no other way to be happy with Jesus but to trust and obey." My grandmother wrote to my mother on her thirtieth birthday with this advice:

> I shall leave you with only a widow's mite when my day of rest comes, but you will claim unknown worlds of joy and satisfaction if you are willing to take from me three little words with which the Lord has blessed and preserved me through dark nights and long days: "Trust and obey."

My mother saw her years of work to publish her mother's writings as an endeavor resting on trust in the Lord. She persevered through long days of disappointment and dark nights of disillusionment because of challenges to her mother's identity and betrayal because of conflict with her family over the royalties. All along she hoped her example, the books she published, and the book she wanted to write about her mother would encourage people to persevere and not to give up on their dreams.

For three years after my grandmother's death, my mother repeatedly tried to take the first steps recounting the journey to publish *O Ye Jigs & Juleps!* and the other books. She gathered her notes in a file called "Ah, Dear Readers." Her story begins,

> From 1954 to 1957, I opened the old suitcase containing the aged ancient dress, a few of the old books, mother's adult religious writings, the childhood essays, but usually they brought back so many memories; bereavement, like so many things in life, you have to learn to live with.

144

Unexpected events slowed my mother's progress, as did the waves of bereavement. My family suffered a serious car accident in October 1956. My parents wanted to visit Thomas Jefferson's home, Monticello. They decided that the history I would absorb on the trip would outweigh whatever I might learn in school that day, an echo of my grandmother's advice a few years before. We set out toward Virginia in the big Mercury. My mother did not drive, and she wanted the most steel around her that we could afford. Her father, Kirtley S. Cleveland, drove "like a bat out of hell," she said, and from that experience she remained a nervous passenger. There were no seat belts or padded dashboards in those days. Heavy rain broke out in the Virginia knolls. As we approached the crest of a hill, a large, dark vehicle hurtled over the top into our lane. It looked as if it was coming through the windshield itself. The impact propelled me forward over the backseat, and I landed headfirst in the front. When I righted myself, I saw dents in the dashboard where my mother's front teeth had been crushed. Her mouth and her head were bleeding. On the other side of the car, the steering wheel was twisted and bent. My father writhed in pain but still gripped and pushed the wheel away from him. He could not move his leg. Sirens blared, and emergency workers transferred my father into an ambulance that roared toward the nearest hospital, in Warrenton, Virginia. After an examination there, an ambulance took us to Prince George's County Hospital near our home in Maryland, where surgeons reconstructed my father's knee. Somehow my mother, dazed and head wrapped in bandages, reached our family dentist's office with me, and he set out to repair and cap her teeth. During my father's lengthy rehabilitation, my mother needed to make arrangements for us to get to the hospital without a car, handle the household, deal with the insurance company, care for my father when he came home, and so much more that I cannot recall.

By the summer of 1957, we set out in a new car to drive west across the country to California. We passed through the Badlands, the lakes of Minnesota, and the mountains of Wyoming and returned via the Grand Canyon and the hot, arid plains of Texas. Inside the soaring castle at Disneyland, the sounds of "When You Wish Upon a Star," the Disney television theme song, lifted my mother's spirit as she wished for a wave of the fairy godmother's wand to publish her mother's writings.

A short while ago, an index card slipped from one of the many folders that hold clippings about *O Ye Jigs & Juleps!* On it, my mother had typed the first nine lines of "The Impossible Dream," the captivating song from *Man of la Mancha*, which roused and delighted Broadway audiences in 1965. I recall attending a performance in Washington, DC, with my parents and Edward, my then boyfriend and now husband. We all sang "The Impossible Dream" as we walked with lilting steps from the theater to the car. By then my mother had realized her dream. Indeed my mother saw the success of the little book as a Cinderella story and yet "a simple, every dayish 'could happen to you' sort of a thing." She mused,

> Like all so called "Cinderella" tales, the ashes and the cinders of the chimney corner are never mentioned, if so, they are seldom heard and oh! so soon, forgotten. These ten little essays SAT in the chimney corner of rejection slips from 1958 to 1961. Several years awaiting a fairy Godmother.

However, when success finally came, its dimensions, not only the delight but also the sorrow, surpassed our imagination. My mother suffered profound disillusionment from attacks on the credibility of my grandmother's writings. She longed to quell all doubts about her mother's authorship of the childhood essays, all due to the originals lost in the 1952 fire. That people doubted her mother's very existence was even harder to bear! How she would have loved access to Google and other electronic resources we have now. My mother began to organize materials for "Ah, Dear Readers" and to pound again on her 1908 typewriter and onionskin carbons. The opening paragraphs for my mother's story of publishing *O Ye Jigs & Juleps!*, a preface of sorts, note first that "a few who have heard the happenings behind the little book have requested this publication for the eyes of many." The opening then tells of a clergyman working in an Episcopal church in Upper Marlboro, Maryland, who read an early draft of my mother's account and remarked that he thought "the explanations contained in this story answered many questions, thus forming a sequel of answers to *O Ye Jigs & Juleps!*"

The start of my mother's focused writing was delayed again by moving from Maryland to Florida in 1971 and then resettling twice in Florida. The condominium my parents chose in Pompano Beach in 1972 had a long living room. At one end, my mother arranged a large table, piled with cascading folders, each tied with knotted string and filled with newspaper clippings and onionskin carbons, all centered by her old typewriter, protected under its cracked plastic cover. The worktable's piles were distinctly purposeful, the tight strings of their folders markedly resolute. The carbon on her fingers caused eye problems, and she began to work wearing gloves.

When I first saw the piles on the table, I asked, "What is all this?" Her eyes lit up with a sparkling sadness, and with her eyebrows arched upward, she answered, "Ah, Dear Readers!" She was working on her story of publishing her mother's writings. I resolved multiple times to help her with writing the book. Life brings interruptions for even the most desired plans. I finished my doctorate, not without delays caused by five surgeries in the 1970s and early 1980s. Eventually I had a computer to use, and I thought that my mother could just write her story and send it to me. I would type what she wrote, make suggestions, and send it to her. Then she would make corrections, and I would enter them. Bang! We would have a chapter in a month or less.

I imagined long sessions, cheerful and tearful, where we would move from memory to tape to computer, writing her story and assembling the remainder of my grandmother's writings—more essays, letters to me, poems, the scrapbook she made when I was five years old. My daughter, Kathleen, born in 1977, would play near us, I thought, and absorb the love of her grandmother, the memory of her great-grandmother, the family stories, and the love of words and writing that extends across generations. I lived in Connecticut then, where my husband, Edward, had his first professorship and Kathleen was born, but we spent extended time with my parents on visits at our home or in Florida. We moved back to the Boston area in 1980, the last year of Jimmy Carter's presidency, when mortgage rates were skyrocketing to over 18 percent. Despite that, we found a small house with a bedroom to accommodate visiting grandparents.

Sometime in the mid-1980s, 1985 to the best of my memory, my soul trembled with the painful awareness that my mother was not well. When we visited Florida at Christmastime, my parents used to take the three of us to Disney World in January, and then we flew home to New England from Orlando. My parents enjoyed Disney World so much that they purchased the annual passes available to Florida residents. They took special delight in the variety of restaurants at Epcot Center. My mother knew very well the pathways from one area to the next. On that trip, however, she lost direction as we entered Epcot. Instead of proceeding directly to the chosen restaurant, she stopped, not knowing where to go. I thought that the lapse was due to fatigue; she tired unusually quickly that year. After I returned home, letters and phone conversations with her revealed gradual traces of brokenness in her handwriting and rambling in her voice and her thoughts. I tried several times to suggest that we work on the book. Eventually I proposed that I tape her voice over the phone as she recounted her memories. But her awareness and focus declined steadily.

I made one last try. My mother had been invited to deliver a short address at ceremonies honoring a historic site, the Woodward Mansion in Bowie, Maryland. She had labored to achieve its registration as a historic landmark after obtaining the same recognition for the stable of the Bel Air Stud on the old Woodward property. We had lived in a suburban community constructed on the pastures where Gallant Fox, Omaha, Nashua, and other great thoroughbred horses used to roam, and as a horseman's daughter, my mother strove to preserve that piece of racing history. Yet now her health was such that there was no question of her attending the ceremony in Bowie. She was asked to send some remarks to be read in her absence. I offered to type them for her from her handwritten copy or from a tape. The next time I asked, I could not be sure that she remembered the first discussion. I found myself saying, "Maybe she will get better, and I can take down what she remembers, then straighten out the rest later. Maybe she is suffering from extreme fatigue." A few weeks later when she sent a note with a check for my husband's and my birthdays and our wedding anniversary, the fractured writing conveyed the piercing image of a trembling hand. My father called to say that day-to-day life was becoming more difficult for them.

When I saw my mother next on a visit to Florida, her memory was dispersing like ripples of water, carrying remembrances and dreams farther away from the center. She confused her stories and got angry when she was corrected even gently. She was suspicious of questions and did not like me looking around. Nonetheless, I did manage to identify the contents of the cherry chest, handmade for her as a hope chest. In it she stashed manuscript originals, letters, extra books, and legal papers, but she did not want to show me anything at length.

In the autumn of 1985, she fell fully into the grip of paranoia. Her erratic behavior and obsessions caused my father terrible anxiety. I flew to Florida in October to intervene. A wise friend suggested that I take her to a doctor under the pretense of bringing my father for medical help. We went to the family physician, who had arranged a visit with a skilled and gentle psychiatrist. Miraculously, after weeks more of troubling behavior, my mother stated that she was ready to go to a hospital, and my father drove her there immediately. Under the psychiatrist's care, she moved through a series of diminishing fears. Some placed her back in frightening childhood experiences, such as the closet where she and her sister were locked for hours after being kidnapped. In contrast, precise short-term memories faded, with a few exceptions. She retained her love for Venice, her favorite city, and she longed to return there. Her eyes and body danced as she recalled its shimmering magic. She would enter the room with her eyebrows raised in excitement and her footsteps bouncing in what my father called a "hillbilly hop." She waved handfuls of money that she pulled from the mysterious hiding places she had created to stash money for the trip she would never again make.

Once a gleeful sampler of as many restaurants in southeast Florida as possible, my mother now feared leaving the house in the evening. What is more, she would go to only one restaurant during the day: an informal outdoor dining area at a hotel on the Intracoastal Waterway. There she delighted in the view of always busy boats against the clear, warm Florida sky. The waitresses, kind and attentive, came to know her and my father. When Kathleen, Edward, and I visited Florida, we went to that same hotel restaurant every day with my mother and father. We were all grateful that she enjoyed at least that one outing.

During the time spent with my mother at home, conversations grew fainter. Her stories grew fewer, her responses faded, and the silence deepened and lengthened. We kept her company in Florida as she stared at the television set. We agonized from afar and visited whenever possible. Time softened her moods, but lucid conversations gradually vanished. Two or three years passed. My father struggled to take care of her at home, and eventually he had to talk to her about leaving home and entering a full-care facility. My mother responded with the simple message of hopeful faith that her mother had instilled: "Trust and obey," she said. "Jesus wouldn't do that to me, not my Jesus."

On November 16, 1989, a sudden and massive heart attack ended my mother's life and the agony of Alzheimer's. My father's phone call came to me in the afternoon, not long before my daughter returned from school. The suddenness took me back to my grandmother's death. My mother learned from a friend's phone call that my grandmother had died abruptly of a heart attack. I found myself then, not yet seven years old, trying to console my mother's overwhelming grief. This time I had a short while to prepare myself for consoling my daughter. The story that my mother wanted to write stayed in the corners of my mind during the distressing years of her illness. The disease stamped out my vision of working together and sharing memories. I realized that I would have to write my grandmother's biography and my mother's story myself. I attempted to begin it several times after my mother's death in 1989, but the weight of grief became too heavy to continue, and the ever-changing demands of life and health caused numerous delays. At first I gathered materials, took notes, and then checked names and dates with my father, but the timing was not right for me to do any more. It was too early. The grief was too heavy. I put aside my writing.

About twenty-five years have passed, and in my sixties the need to write has pressed harder and harder upon me. I opened the same cherry chest that my mother used. Edward helped me move scrapbooks and photos and letters into working order. I have fulfilled my mother's wish. The biography of Virginia Cary Hudson is done, "Ah, Dear Readers" appears within it, and my scrapbook is published at last in the pages that follow.

Chapter 5

"Enjoy All the Good Things Now": Letters and a Scrapbook for a Granddaughter

My grandmother sent thoughtful letters and charming drawings to bridge the months and the miles between our visits. She also gathered poems and pictures in a scrapbook so that I always had remembrances of her at home. One of the scrapbook poems teaches a lesson that my grandmother passes on from sighing flowers: "'Enjoy me today,' they said, / 'Tomorrow, I shall die.'" Passages from the letters illustrate her lively and loving imagination, her humorous approach to life, and her teachings about life, death, and eternal life. Those themes continue in the scrapbook, where Gammee (the first sounds I made when trying to say Grandma or Grandmother) advises me about making the most of life, as she surely did. A certain sadness, perhaps unexpected in writings for a five-year-old, underlies the poems.

> All things should be enjoyed today,
> that we both hear and see,
> lest we become so sorry,
> when they no longer be.

The Letters to Beverly: From Monkeydom to Young Ladyhood

The first letter I have in my grandmother's hand dates from 1951, before my fourth birthday; the last was written after Valentine's Day in 1954, around two months before she died. She also inserted short notes, poems, and more pictures for me into letters that she mailed to my mother. In 1951, my grandmother's letters call me Beverly, "Monkey," and little Beverly. By July of 1952, she announced in a letter from Wheeling, West Virginia, that "Monkey" no longer suited me:

> Now that you are five years old, I can't call you monkey anymore. You have graduated from monkeydom to young ladyhood. I admit there is little difference. Now, when you go to your room, you are too big to jump from bed to bed, and clatter.

From then on she called me simply Beverly or, as in her last letter, dearest Beverly. She also wrote in the persona of the stick horse Pal to "Pal Beverly" and on behalf of the mouse in the kitchen to "Little Thing." She closed all her letters with "Love, Gammee." Sometimes she added a drawing of herself.

My grandmother's letters reveal her gift for entering the make-believe world of young children. She gave voices to creatures, and she animated objects I knew from her household, her yard, her neighborhood, and places we had visited together. At the "rooster store" in downtown Louisville, she saw "the cutest yellow pussy cat." Her imaginary conversation with the yellow cat about me included her upcoming journey to Johns Hopkins. She created a comic scene with the cat, herself, the doctor, and his needle. The cat "told me when nobody was listening, that he would like to live with you in Bellemeade, so I will bring him up to Johns Hopkins. I bet when the Doctor gets out his long needle, he will jump under the bed. I would too, but I am too fat." On another trip to town, which meant

*Self-portrait by Virginia Cary Hudson Cleveland in a letter
to her granddaughter, Beverly Mayne, 1952*

downtown Louisville, Gammee brought home a stick horse for me. "Town" held all sorts of excitement.

> I can see MORE THINGS when I go in town. Yesterday I saw a stick horse. He had bells on his white bridle. I asked him if he would like to go home with me, to wait for you, and I was just sure that I heard him say "thank you very much." Coming home I stood him up in the taxi, so that he could see out of the window. You can take him out to the stable, and gallop him up and down under the shed row. I am sure the other horses will like him very much. I don't believe that I would enter him in the Derby, if I were you, because it will make him too tired, and too nervous. I will let you name him.

Pal, the name I gave the stick horse, could take me on gallops around the house and even in the stable, and he could talk to the horses at Churchill Downs. But make-believe had limits: racing Pal at the track would not be possible.

Squirrels ran to and fro across St. James Court, scampering up the old trees. One squirrel became an imaginary friend and asked my grandmother about me: "The little squirrel was on the front steps this morning. He asked me when you were coming back, and I told him very soon, and he said 'good.'" Once the squirrel seemed quite sad over my absence, but my grandmother assured him that I would return. "The little squirrel sits under the pink swing, and looks and looks and looks for you. I told him not to cry, that you would be back." The squirrel addressed me in a letter.

> Hello Beverly,
>
> How are you? I am well, I thank you. Toodle doodle doo.

Gammee is going to buy me some peanuts today. I miss you very much.

The peanuts cheered up the squirrel as well as his friends, she said. "I took a big old gourd, and filled it with peanuts for the squirrel. He told all of his friends, and they are out there now jumping and eating, just as fast as they can."

Gammee promised me a duck to play with when I came to visit

Drawing of a squirrel in a letter from Virginia Cary Hudson Cleveland to her granddaughter, Beverly Mayne, 1952. The squirrel is signing a letter to Beverly.

and recorded the steps to fulfilling the promise in a few following letters. The spring after my tonsils were removed, she wrote about the duck: "I will not forget what I told you about the duck I am going to have for you. You can be thinking up a good name for him." Then one day, when coming home from the Goodwill Chapel, she found the duck.

> And coming along on my way home, what do you think I saw? A little duck! A promise is a promise. I told you I would have one when you came next time. He sits in his little box, and looks out of the windows I have cut for him. Maybe he is looking for you. I told him you would be here … Good, you be thinking of a name for your duck, and when you come, he will follow you and Honey Hug [my name for my father] all around. Honey Hug will just love that. And with your new coat on, and your duck going along too, you will look just too ducky.

Pal, the stick horse, joined the conversation and told me in his letter that the duck grew tired from looking and waiting for my arrival: "Donald gets tired waiting for you to come, then he stretches out and goes to sleep." An update from Gammee on the duck read,

I thought that maybe you would like to know how your duck is getting along. Every morning he swims in the dish pan, then he sits in his rocking chair and rocks, while I fix his breakfast. Then he eats, and when I put his box in the sun, he puts his head under his wings, and goes to sleep. Then I tip around so that I won't wake him up.

Sometime later my grandmother let me know that Donald was getting too big for his surroundings: "Donald has grown up so much, that he is too big for his rocking chair. When you come I will have some rubber pants for him, so that he can sit in your lap, and rock in the big rocking chair." Gammee waited for me to come so that we could bring him to the duck pond together. I remember riding in the car to a park in Louisville, letting him out, and watching him waddle over to the pond. My grandmother and I had a long talk about doing what was best for Donald, given his nature as a duck. I was sad but accepting. I worried about him and wondered if he wanted to return to St. James Court and to his rocking chair. My grandmother visited him and sent reports on his well-being. Once he followed her when he saw her at the pond's edge, but shortly he adjusted. She wrote, "You will remember that I promised you that I would go out and see about Donald. He knew me alright, but this time he did not want to come home with me. He has gotten to like the other ducks very much, and he ran and got in the water to show me what a fine swimmer and diver he has become." Donald was excelling as a duck in his swimming and diving. Raising him taught me a lesson about the needs and nature of nonhuman creatures and about keeping promises, affirming achievements, and making decisions together for the well-being of another.

A tiny mouse that took shelter in the warm house felt my absence just as my grandmother did: "A Little Mouse lives in the kitchen and dances on the biscuit board. He says for me to tell you hello and for you to come to Kentucky to see him very soon." The beaten biscuit board would have been a perfect hiding place for a mouse. The board, also called a brake, consisted of "a pair of steel rollers geared together and operated by a hefty crank, mounted on a small table with a marble top and cast iron legs."[164] My grandmother's beaten biscuit board had a low shelf underneath the marble top, where a mouse could conceal itself. My husband and I kept the weighty board for decades, finally leaving it behind when we changed to condominium living. It provided the perfect surface for rolling out any kind of dough.

The real and the imaginary animated not only the mouse's habitat but also the Ohio River in Wheeling, where my grandmother penned a letter from a hotel:

> On the river are all kinds of boats. Little ones that honk, bigger ones that toot, and real big ones that blow just as loud as they can ... There are two big bridges over the River, and people just come and go, and come and go, all day, and all night. I bet these rascals haven't made up their beds, or washed one dish. They don't even have time to cook. Maybe they eat popsicles, and throw the sticks in the river for the fish to use for oars, when they ride in their little bark boats. If I see one going by, I will tell you.

Gammee's depiction of the river moves from the large bridges and the boats to the fish rowing in make-believe boats made from the bark of tree limbs that fall into the water. What is more, my grandmother imagined how she would feel if she were a boat. She then returned to reality, describing how she would get into the river as a human:

> I don't think I would like to be a boat, and have my bottom wet, all the time. I am going to tell you a secret. I am going to drive your grandaddy's car right down to the very edge of the water. Then, I am going to take off my shoes and stockings, and open the door, and WADE. A horse that was born in May,

will lie down in the water every chance he gets, as
long as he lives; I was born in May but I wear clothes,
so I can't get down and roll, I have to just WADE.

Horses often served as a frame of reference for human activity
and vice versa, as seen in how my grandmother identified with
horses born in May that loved to get into the water. In another letter
she explained horse behavior in human terms.

I got this paper especially to write to you on. It
came from the airport, where we went to see the
Buckleys off to Hot Springs. Mrs. Buckley says that
Tom Fool doesn't want any children. They brought
some beautiful mares to be his bride, so that he could
raise a family, and Tom Fool was bored to death,
and stood right up and went to sleep. Your Mother
always thought that Tom Fool was smart, now she
will think that he is smarter than ever. Even Mr.
Webster's dictionary, when you are old enough to
have one, won't quite explain the meaning of Mr.
Whitney's frustration. It would take somebody from
Ky to fully understand that, and Mr. Webster was
a Yankee, so there are many things which he just
wouldn't know.

Mr. Buckley, my grandfather's business partner, apparently bought
brood mares to breed for a hefty fee with Tom Fool, Horse of the
Year in 1953, retired to stud at Greentree Stable, which was owned
by the well-known Whitney family. Tom Fool's reluctance to mate
cost Mr. Whitney the stud fees. Breeding horses, big business in
Kentucky, frequently occupied the center of conversations in horse-
racing circles. My grandmother used the importance of the subject
to take a jab at northerners. Whether I understood any of what she
said, I do not know, but I wonder now if she intended to push my
mother into teaching a basic lesson on the "birds and bees" earlier
than she would have otherwise.

Another famous thoroughbred gave the name to one of my toy stuffed horses, and the play horse experienced a make-believe version of what ailed the real horse. Hill Gail won the 1952 Kentucky Derby when an ill Tom Fool was unable to race. Hill Gail was injured during the race, and so was my Hill Gail. Gammee made sure I had what was needed to take care of him.

> I think that Hill Gail would like to have a pillow, because the newspaper says that he is sick. So I took a corner of an oat's bag, from a real racing stable, and made him a pillow case. And what could be nicer, and softer, to stuff it with, then cotton drifting down from the top of my tree! Your mother will sew it up for you.
>
> Now, when Hill Gail goes to sleep he can dream about bright sunshine, and clouds looking down, and a million little leaves fanning him, to keep him nice and cool. Isn't that cute?

Hill Gail soon after received a blanket, just like a real horse would have. My grandmother made it out of an old horse blanket, yellow with black strips as decoration, just as she did for my other play horse, Market Level, named for my grandfather's stakes winner. In late May, Gammee wrote, "Today you should get the blankets I made for Market Level, and Hill Gail. I hope that you like them. By now I guess that you have gotten the pillow for Hill Gail. Market Level doesn't need one, because he is not sick." Oats bags or feed sacks nonetheless found many uses in our household. I still had one until a few years ago when it finally wore out.

My grandmother gave feelings to objects as well as living creatures. Even the sled had sentiments of its own; she wrote, "It has snowed and snowed this winter, and the sled down in the basement looked out the dirty basement window and said it wished to goodness that you were here so it could take you for a ride. The sled sits by itself downstairs, and I sit by myself upstairs." The ticktock living room clock sounded its thoughts: "I sit by the fire and the clock talks to me. It tells me all the places it would like to go and all the things it would like to do." The fish, in contrast, kept silent company: "I have some fish in the bowl and they don't do anything but swim. I listen, and listen, and they never say a word." Later the same day, my grandmother added a postscript to a letter sent to my mother: "Tell Beverly the fish are named Swimmie, Finnie, and Minnie." Outside the house, the grass emerging in spring felt the rake's movement. "The green grass is coming up after being asleep so long under the snow. Today I am going to rake the ugly old rubbish out of it, so it can grow. I bet the grass will think that feels good. Just like having your back scratched."

In 1953, after I received my new collapsible doll buggy for Christmas, I left my old one at my grandparents' house. My grandmother reported on the first buggy, bringing it to life with a letter from the carriage itself.

> Hello, Beverly,
>
> How are you? I am well. I thank you. Toodle, doodle, doo. I sit in the dining room. I am very lonesome. Sometimes the sun comes in and shines on the floor. Sometimes he forgets. When the dust mop comes along, I roll out of his way. I go to the grocery, but I am sad because you are not there to go with me.

The lonesome carriage gives its view of the household—whether or not the sun shines on the floor, moments when the mop enters its space, and trips outside to the grocery. Missing me, though, is the strongest emotion it expresses.

Also lonesome for me was

Drawing of the buggy carriage in a letter from Virginia Cary Hudson Cleveland to her granddaughter, Beverly Mayne, 1952. The buggy carriage sits alone and misses Beverly.

an all-day sucker, and my grandmother gave it a voice too. I loved sweets, any kind of sweets, and I wiggled and squealed with delight when Gammee bought me a sweet, pink, sticky all-day sucker. I called it a googie. My mother explained to me when I was older that sometimes my grandmother would call on the phone and say she was "the googie." My eyes would get as big as saucers. A special all-day sucker joined the Louisville make-believe world and sent me a letter.

> Hello Beverly,
>
> How are you? I am well. I thank you. Toodle, doodle, doo. My number is 222. I am very lonesome, for no one ever calls me on the telephone any more.

My grandmother also promised to bring a googie to Maryland if she could. She wrote,

> I am coming to see you, and I will have to ride and ride and ride, I will stop and eat, and eat, and drink Coca Cola, and then drink some more Coca Cola. If I see some googies sitting by the road, I will say 'Good Morning Mr. Googie, would you like to go to Beverly's house?' They will say 'yes, thank you very much,' and I will bring them with me.

Drawing of a sucker candy, or "googie," in a letter from Virginia Cary Hudson Cleveland to Beverly Mayne, 1952. The all-day sucker misses Beverly.

Pal, the stick horse that wrote to me about Donald, promised to wait faithfully until I arrived one year.

> Dear Pal Beverly,
>
> I just keep on waiting. I am standing up by the big chest, looking out of the window for you, and I

am going to stand right here, and watch for you until you come. Yesterday it snowed, and my nose against the cold glass made me shiver. I hope that you will take me out to Churchill Downs with you to see my horse cousins. Maybe they will tell me which one is going to win, and then I can tell you, then we will all have some money. Goody, goody.

Hurry, and love from your Pal, the Stick-Horse

In the Kentucky make-believe world my grandmother created, Pal's horse appearance made him a sort of intermediary; he would talk to the horses at the racetrack and then to me. Pal would

Drawing of Pal, the Stick-Horse, in a letter from Virginia Cary Hudson Cleveland to Beverly Mayne, 1952. Pal, the Stick-Horse, waits for Beverly to go to the races.

discover which horse planned on winning and tell me, and I would take care of placing the winning bet. The big chest where Pal rested eventually made the journey north with other furniture to my home, but we parted with it when we moved into a condominium.

Letters and drawings from my grandmother remain treasured gifts. She also mailed presents, specially purchased for me, such as an Easter outfit. She located items one at a time on various shopping trips and described each one as she found it.

Yesterday I trimmed your Easter bonnet. It is straw, and a dress is in the box now too. When I get socks, pants, and a petticoat, and gloves, I will mail it. Am working on Auntie Ann to put in five dollars, so your mother can get some patent leather slippers. Tell her to have your blue coat cleaned, and not to put it off.

If she doesn't get it out and send it this minute, you
spank her for me.

Letter by letter and shopping trip by shopping trip, the outfit came
together, and the excitement built up over the sending and the arrival
of the packages. The Easter bonnet arrived with a poem in which the
flowers on the hat introduce themselves and send good wishes.

I'm a bright red poppy
In Flander's field, I live.
And I'm a blue cornflower
Good Luck to you, I'll give.
And best of all—a daisy
I grow in hills and dells
And if you are naughty—ooh—
A daisy NEVER tells!
And last of all a rosebud
on your ribbon sits, and swings;
and hopes this little bonnet,
a happy Easter to you brings.

My mother wrote to my grandmother as soon as the pretty outfit
arrived, and Gammee wrote in return, delighted that her choices
were appreciated. My grandmother ensured that a piece of clothing
she chose and sent to me would feel like a part of herself that I would
receive and cherish.

Gratitude was one of the lessons about life that her letters taught
me. Another was that females were often put in second place behind
men. From a hotel window in Wheeling, she explained, "I live in
this big house, way up high, where I have marked the window. In
front of the house is a big river. Old Man River. He has been there
for thousands of years." His female counterpart, she noted, was
never mentioned, but she explained how Mrs. River's seniority
increased her status: "Nobody ever says anything about Mrs. River.
I guess she was older than her husband and dried up long ago."

My grandmother prepared me for big events, such as having my tonsils removed in Louisville during Christmas vacation. In describing the hospital she mixed the humorously real and the storybook imaginary. She also devised a game to practice before surgery.

> I am going to tell you about the hospital you are going to in Louisville. It is the Ice Cream Hospital. That's because they let you have all the ice cream you can eat and that's where they get rid of those old sore tonsils. It will be very early in the morning, too early for the Doctor to get dressed, so he will have on his white night shirt and a night cap to match. In story books, people wore night caps. This Doctor is old, and I guess he might have lived in story book days, because he still has his night cap. I bet he took out Cinderella's and Little Red Riding Hood's tonsils. Then he will have on his rubber gloves so his hands will feel soft, and his finger nails can't scratch. Then he will have on a mask, to keep the germs away. Germs are little things that fly around and nobody can see them except fairies and brownies. And the Doctor is not a brownie, and I hope he isn't a fairy so he can't see them. So he wears his mask and all you can see is his eyes. He will look so cute! I bet you will want to laugh when you see him. And the nurse will be all dressed up in her new white shoes. She doesn't know that white shoes in the winter time are tacky. And she isn't going to let the Doctor get ahead of her, so she is going to have on a cap, too. Then they will put you up on a table. That will be fun. When I was a little girl I used to sit on a table and put my bare toes in the butter. It felt so squashy and cool. I liked that. Then they will have a little cap for you, a rubber one, but instead of putting it on your head, you wear it on your nose, of all things, but that's so you can smell it. And you smell, and smell, and it's a sleeping smell. Did you ever look at a cloud drifting

in the sky and wonder how much fun it would be to drift, and wonder how it looked, way up there? A lot better than riding in a plane. That's what the sleeping smell does. It makes you feel just like a cloud, and you will feel so good. And when you wake up your tonsils will be gone!

My grandmother turned the Louisville doctor into a character who could move from reality to make-believe. Storybook characters, she assured me, endured the real necessity of having their tonsils out, while germs were visible only to make-believe figures such as fairies and brownies (little elves). She likened the dreadful smell of ether and its effects to drifting like a cloud. Perhaps that image lessened my fear, but I still remember the taste of ether and the swirling feeling that followed sniffing it.

My grandmother turned the need not to swallow after surgery into a game that I could practice before getting to the hospital and could use to tease my mother.

The only thing to remember is not to swallow, but just spit. You might practice up on your spitting out in the yard. A good spitting game, if you want to play it, is gargling ... This is how you play it. You put a little, not too much, just a little lemonade in your mouth, and when it tries to go down, you try to keep it up. And you will make the funniest noise. A lot more fun than sucking on a straw. When you suck you swallow, anybody can do that. But when you gargle, you don't swallow. You just jump the lemonade up and down and then see how far you can spit it out. When you learn to gargle, you can learn to spit *real* far, all over the sink, and maybe up on the window. And that would be funny. You get Honey Hug to practice the gargle game with you. It's a funny game, and see which one of you can spit the highest. Your mother will love that.

The gargling-and-spitting game probably succeeded at preparing me not to swallow and certainly at aggravating my mother enormously. What could be more unladylike than a spitting daughter!

Serious lessons about life entered some letters. My grandmother introduced the reality of death when she reported that someone outside the family had passed away and gone to heaven: "He has gone to heaven to live with God. No more rent, no more groceries, no more taxes, and no more gasoline." She described the next world as a place for fun and then imagined herself there, playing a harp.

> Everybody has wings and they can fly where they are going. And old Saint Peter says, "Hi, Toots" and God says, "You finally made it, good for you." And Jesus gives you a beautiful crown and a golden harp. I know what I'M going to play on mine if I ever get one. I am going to play "Dixie." I sure am going to have fun when I am dead. I hope!

Eternal life appeared in several letters when Gammee taught me about church and about some events in the liturgical year. Her remark that "church is where you learn about God and everlasting life" continued with an evocation of flying angels. She imagined herself in the scene enjoying heavenly benefits: "If I ever get to be an angel, this is how I will look, and I will fly real high over the oceans, around the world, and wave at the sea gulls and the

Virginia's drawing of herself as an angel with wings and tail feathers for Beverly Mayne, 1952

eagles and say 'Pooh O says-the-dog!'" In her drawing, a somewhat wild-looking angel extends her wings and boasts tail feathers. The angel exclaims, "All God's chillun got wings and some got tail feathers too." With wings outstretched, the angel flies exuberantly across the bottom of the letter. Her picture in flight surely brought giggles to her granddaughter.

Writing from Canada, my grandmother described the scenery and imagined angels dangling their toes in the beautiful lake: "Where I live, up here, I can see the Lake, and way far off the sky comes down and touches the water. I bet the angels fly real low and drag their toes in the waves. I mustn't forget to try it, if I ever get to be an angel." She also explained the difference between an angel and a hant, an old word for ghost: "I will be looking for you in Kentucky in October. Maybe Devil's Grin will be there, too. He is as fast as a 'hant.' A hant is first cousin to an angel. The angel has wings. The hant doesn't need them." Poor Devil's Grin the racehorse perished in the 1952 fire at Wheeling's Waterford Park.

Churchgoers do not all seem destined for wings. She warned me about the pretentious. "I am going to church today to slice ham for the lumuxes to eat," she commented. "A lumux is a dressed up nobody who thinks she is somebody." Gammee visited other churches, however, where lumuxes had no sway. In one letter she empathized with the troubled who were nonetheless wiser due to suffering, and she taught compassion:

> This morning I went down on skid-row. That is where the poor, and crippled, and blind people are. And a little church is down there, and when the bell rings, at noon, the bums come in off the street, and that is where I go to tell them things about God. You see when people have had a lot of trouble, they find out a lot of things, like I have, that other people ought to know. That makes things easier for them.

In other writings, my grandmother recounted her experiences at the Goodwill Chapel and the Salvation Army Chapel in Louisville.

The audience was far more diverse than the folks at Calvary Episcopal Church, and she touched their hearts with her strong faith, her direct compassionate speech, and her ability to laugh at herself. She accepted tough preaching jobs there such as Lent and Good Friday.

After Easter, my grandmother wrote, "In forty more days is Ascension Day. Your mother will tell you what that means, and I have drawn you a picture, so you won't forget." The picture is indeed memorable. A long-bearded God, wearing a crown and smoking a pipe, remarks, "Welcome home, Kid," as a young, bearded Jesus, halo floating over his head, rises amid a shining cluster of clouds with his bare feet dangling down above the Mount of Olives. The Sea of Galilee extends across the foreground, and a tiny bird perches in the tree at the lower left. Jesus bids farewell to the world below and his followers, promising, "Don't cry, I'll be back some day." Three years later Gammee departed the world herself, without time to say farewell.

Drawing of the Ascension for Beverly Mayne, included in a letter from Virginia Cary Hudson Cleveland to her daughter, Virginia Cleveland Mayne, 1952. In the drawing Jesus ascends over the Mount of Olives and returns to heaven.

My Scrapbook

My grandmother brought the scrapbook to me in July 1953, after a June stay at Johns Hopkins for kidney treatments. The scrapbook poems describe St. James Court and its surroundings—objects and creatures that converse and express feelings, as they do in my grandmother's letters to me. A little flower listens to people talk and finds their words trivial. A blue bird offers a lesson on happiness and troubles. An owl discusses its view on life in a tree. The pink swing, the ants in the yard, the moss on the rock, and a vine in the garden all say, "We're all just waiting for a little girl / to come back here to play." Gammee describes my bed in her house from my point of view: "When I visit in Kentucky, / I sleep in a little bed / ... If I get much bigger / in this bed I cannot sleep. / Up and over the foot board / I'll have to hang my feet."

In contrast, the beautiful fountain in St. James Court has no feelings: "She can't see, nor hear, nor feel, / nor think, nor even die." My grandmother concludes about the lovely lady, "I'm glad the fountain lady is she, / And I'm glad that I am I." As president of the St. James Court Association for more than eight years, my grandmother struggled to maintain the fountain and its lady, which Mr. Slaughter had brought from England when he designed St. James Court, the year after the 1887 Louisville Exposition.

My grandmother's poems advise me how to treat friends and neighbors. She cites the motto from the Bristol school, "where pomp and grandeur walked the halls," in a poem as she does in her letters and essays: "Politeness is to do and say, / the kindest thing, in the kindest way." No matter how much you learn in school, she warns, "You have not learned a thing of worth, / unless you learn to be polite." A pragmatic concern underlies a poem on neighbors. My grandmother hides when she hears a knock, because she has grown tired of her neighbor. But what if the neighbor did the same if my grandmother needed her? She concludes with a lesson inspired by the Golden Rule: "I had better run, to let her in, / in haste across my floor. / My need may very urgent be, / when I knock on her door."

My grandmother teaches me about faith and thanksgiving in her poems. God's presence manifests itself everywhere. The stars signify God's blessings, and the rainbow offers a sign of hope. God created these visible gifts and the capabilities of our living bodies: "God regulates your breathing. / He gives you hearing and sight. / How about taking a little time, / to thank Him every night?" A portrait of the Madonna accompanies a poem that expresses reverence for Mary the mother of Jesus and that counsels all to treat their mothers well.

In "The Finish," Gammee makes an extended comparison between the race of life and horse racing. "God looks down on the Race of Life" and knows the difficulties you meet. "He knows what odds are against you, / and when your feet slip in Life's mud. / He knows the difference in going that's tough / and a track that is fast and good." God will be a kind judge at the end of life, and unlike the results at the racetrack, "'The last shall be first,' He plainly tells you, / and also, 'The first shall be last.'"

A humorous but sharp longing for equality between men and women comes to light in my grandmother's comments on working and wearing pants like a man: "It's wonderful to be a man, / and walk with your pants showing." Women my age remember well what Joan Collins recounts in her book on the breakthrough for women in the 1960s. Collins opens with the famous 1960 incident when Lois Rabinowitz arrived at traffic court in New York City to pay a ticket for her boss. She was wearing pants, and the judge sent her out. Lois had her husband pay the ticket and promised to "go home and burn all [her] slacks." In 1972, Felix Frankfurter rejected Ruth Bader Ginsburg's application for a clerkship at the Supreme Court and remarked, "I can't stand girls in pants." By 2007, pants were the norm for certain jobs, and Tahita Jenkins was fired from her post as a bus driver in New York City because she refused to wear them.[165]

Changes were coming in the 1960s to combat bias against women and discrimination against African Americans. In late 1952 or 1953, my grandmother described her household worker Mary

Belle as having dark skin because God took extra time to color her face black. She reminds in one of her poems that a man of color, Joseph of Arimathea, carried Jesus's cross, and "That's more than a white man did." Nonetheless, she sees bearing "the weight of the world" as the lot of African Americans as long as they live. No hope for change and no anticipation of the next decade appear here. However, in a letter from Las Vegas (October 6, 1953), she observed with no disapproval that there was "no segregation" where she was eating. While she "was eating soup at the Round Up, the Mills Brothers were eating ham sandwiches and drinking ale, at the next table." In 1953, the Mills Brothers, a group of four singers known for their version of "Tiger Rag," "Dinah," "You Always Hurt the One You Love," "Lazy River," and other songs, were performing in Las Vegas at the Thunderbird, which was sold later and called El Rancho.[166]

As for my family members, the scrapbook depicts them in humorous or lighthearted scenes. My mother "hates to cook, and hates to clean, / but how she loves her flowers!" My father "loves me when I'm all waked up" and "loves me while I sleep." My auntie "pecks on her typewriter" and "shops and says, 'Just charge it,' / And then she moans and groans." Auntie did love to shop, and she extended her generosity to me and my family, from the appliances for our house to airfare for research conferences before I had university funds to special outfits for all of us to wear. My grandfather ate "five times a day," beginning with two to three breakfasts around the morning workouts for the horses. He would sit and read "his racing form, with his face screwed in a knot." My father's mother "earns her money, / just like any man." My grandmother Mayne taught in a one-room schoolhouse in Iowa and then worked for the federal government in Washington, DC, until her retirement.

Animals, like humans, differ in their spirit. My grandmother uses two poems to illustrate the contrasting dispositions of Rory, an Irish setter who lived in Louisville, and Sambo, my mother's cocker spaniel who moved from Kentucky to Maryland. Rory demonstrated obedience and gentleness, while Sambo, known for scaring all the neighborhood dogs and biting me, possessed a terrible temperament. Perhaps he resented moving.

My grandmother Virginia tells a delightfully imaginative tale in one scrapbook poem, probably inspired by the Harrowing of Hell, Christ's descent into hell to free the souls trapped there. She imagines herself as an angel who "skips down a moonbeam." The blazing fires do not burn her, because she dons asbestos boots, pinches the devil, and then rings a fire bell. A long hose descends, and she extinguishes the fires with the result that:

> The gamblers will run for the races.
> The thieves will grab up their loot.
> The liars, and cheats, will shout, three cheers,
> for the angel from Heaven, in asbestos boots!

The poems contain other treasures that I leave the reader to discover. The poem "One Day" in my scrapbook expresses my grandmother's hope that something I found there would hold enough value for me that I would pass it on to others. Indeed I have done both, the valuing and the passing on. My grandmother would be thrilled that her poems are being read, for she wrote:

> These rhymes may now
> quite senseless seem,
>
> but one day you'll know
> what they mean.
> If in them you find anything
> to pass on to another.
> The one who will be very proud
> will be your old Grandmother.

Together the letters, poems, and drawings that my grandmother made for me offer lessons about life, its blessings, its sorrows, its injustices, and practical lessons on how to treat neighbors. They teach about the church and the meaning of the liturgical year, about nature with the change of seasons, and about love for animals, who have feelings and voices. She was always able to laugh at herself. The world my grandmother animated in the letters and the scrapbook kept memories alive and expressed deep love, whether longing to be together, joyous anticipation at a coming reunion, or sadness after separation. Now when I am over sixty, I can still feel the loving essence of a grandmother I knew fewer than seven years.

The following pages contain the poems and drawings Gammee made for me when I was approaching my sixth birthday. The scrapbook with writings from her childhood and her family history perished in the October 1952 fire. Once the house became livable again, she sat down to make a new scrapbook, to present the world to a five-year-old in fanciful poems and drawings that would generate healing laughter to soothe the grief over losing aged treasures. Yet sadness and the heaviness of illness pierce through the lessons she taught me in the scrapbook's poems and drawings. My grandmother's sense of aging and time swiftly passing proved accurate. She lived less than a year beyond the summer of 1953, when she brought the scrapbook to me in Maryland.

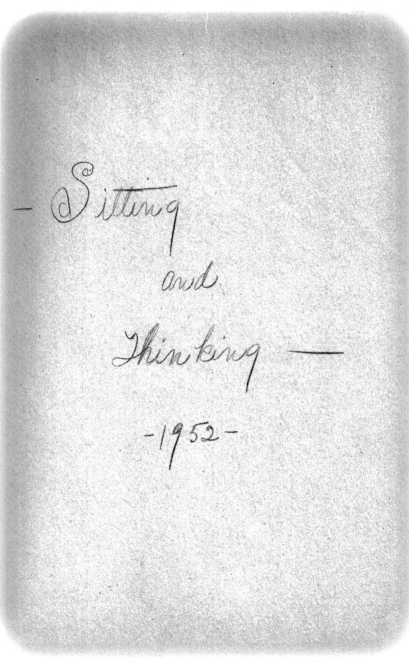

Cover of scrapbook, "Sitting and Thinking," 1952

"A Red Bird" illustration by Virginia Cary Hudson Cleveland, 1953

A Red Bird

I saw a red bird
sitting on a limb.
He said "hello" to me.
I said "hello" to him.
I said, "Where do you go
when it is time to snow?"
He said, "Listen if you
really want to know;
I go down South
where it is nice and warm. I fly all the way,
because my wings are strong."
Now I can't go along,
and here's the reason why;
I'm not a red bird,
and I can't fly.
I'll sit by the fire,
and wait for Springtime.
My not having any wings
was God's idea, not mine.

"A Little Flower" illustration by Virginia Cary Hudson Cleveland, 1953

A LITTLE FLOWER

I am a little flower.
I live in Gammee's pot.
I listen to the people talk.
I never heard such rot.
They worry over silly things
they can not know, and see,
the things that really matter
are things like God, and me.

SMILE

If you are too much in a hurry,
you'll always fail to see,
the little flower beside the road,
the leaves upon the tree.
If you, thru life, more slowly go,
and take time out to smile,
you'll find so very many things
to make it more worth while.

THE DIPPER

God holds in His hand, a dipper of stars,
filled with blessings, intended for you.
He will pour them out, before your eyes,
if you are unselfish, and true.

"A Blue Bird" illustration by Virginia Cary Hudson Cleveland, 1953

A Blue Bird

I saw a blue bird,
perched up high
resting there
against the sky.
"I am Happiness,"
he said to me.
I thought, "Happiness,
where can you be?"
He said, "Here am I,
don't let trouble blind you.
If you turn your eyes away,
you will never find me."

Raindrops

Did you ever watch the raindrops
stream down the window glass,
like tears upon a lady's cheek?
None of them will last.
The sun will dry the raindrops.
A kiss can dry the tears.
All things in this world pass away,
including all our fears.

School

Soon you will be in a school
to learn to read and write,
and while you're learning many things,
of this do not lose sight.
You have not learned a thing of worth,
unless you learn to be polite.
Politeness is a magic charm,
a soothing salve, a healing balm.
Once I went away to school,
where pomp and grandeur walked the halls.
I saw a glowing motto there,
in gold, upon one of the walls.
"Politeness is to do and say,
the kindest thing, in the kindest way."
I was in search of music, language,
literature, and art,
and there I found this simple truth
with which my life to start.

A Rainbow

Did you ever see a rainbow?
If you never did, you will.
The best place to see one
is high upon a hill.
When you're way down
in the dumps,
you'll never see
a thing but bumps.
You have to raise your hopes, and eyes,
to see a rainbow
in the skies.

Thanks

Thank God for all the '50 Fords.
Thank God for fields and clover.
Thank God for Honey-Hugs and home.
Thank God for Coca-Cola!

THE DOUBLE RING CEREMONY

It's wonderful to be a man,
and walk with your pants showing.
To get paid for all your time,
without housework, or sewing.
In addition to these torments,
the women have the babies.
"Ain't" that something, God have mercy
on all travailing ladies!
Now isn't there just some way,
to get even with a man?
You bet there is; I'll marry one
and seal him in a can.
With a ring upon his finger,
that every one can see,
and another in his nose,
to be pulled and jerked by me.

EVERY DAY

Every day was made for fun.
That makes all days Fundays.
Some folks think God sleeps all week,
and just wakes up on Sundays.
They think He lives inside a church.
They're crazy! They can't see,
that God is in all things He made,
even you and me.

GRATITUDE

God regulates your breathing.
He gives you hearing and sight.
How about taking a little time,
to thank Him every night?

THE FOUNTAIN LADY

I know a fountain in Saint James Court
where a lady stands up high.
She can't see, nor hear, nor feel,
nor think, nor even die.
Without these things, what is the use
to lift her face up to the sky?
I'm glad the fountain lady is she,
And I'm glad that I am I.

"In Kentucky" illustration by Virginia Cary Hudson Cleveland, 1953

In Kentucky

When I visit in Kentucky,
I sleep in a little bed.
I pull the covers up to my chin
and on a pillow
I place my head.
If I get much bigger
in this bed I cannot sleep.
Up and over the foot board
I'll have to hang my feet.

"A Little Owl" illustration by Virginia Cary Hudson Cleveland, 1953

A LITTLE OWL

I have a little owl,
and he said to me,
"How would you like to live
with me, here in my tree?"
And I said, "Fine,
except for the rain."
And he said, "Now
isn't it a shame,
you don't have a feather-coat,
and can't sit with me,
when the rain comes down,
high up in my tree."

"A Yard" illustration by Virginia Cary Hudson Cleveland, 1953

A YARD

There is a yard, a beautiful yard,
where the grass grows green and soft.
Everywhere are the busy ants,
and on a rock is some moss.
There's a pink swing there, and a vine grows low.
And each of them seems to say,
"We're all just waiting for a little girl
to come back here to play."

MY MOTHER

I have a darling mother.
Outdoors she'll work for hours.
She hates to cook, and hates to clean,
but how she loves her flowers!
When she is mad, she cracks her heels,
and stomps first in, then out.
I bet she doesn't know herself,
what she is mad about!

MY DADDY

I have a big tall daddy.
God gave him to me to keep.
He loves me when I'm all waked up.
He loves me while I sleep.
I climb into his big, strong lap,
and then I feel so snug.
You think his name is Lewis,
but I know it's "Honey Hug."

MY AUNTIE ANN

I have a little Auntie,
and her little name is Ann.
She pecks on her typewriter
as fast as ever she can.
She shops and says, "Just charge it."
And then she moans and groans.
Does anybody know a place
where she can get some loans?

HOME

I have a house, a little house,
but it's big enough for me.
With a stove to cook and a chair to sit,
and a bed for each of us three.
It is the nicest little house
that every there could be.
Best of all, it is my home
'cause Love lives there with me.

GRANDADDY

I have an old Grandaddy
who eats five times a day.
He stirs in corn, and oats, and bran,
and walks on straw, and hay.
He sits and reads his racing form,
with his face screwed in a knot.
And if you ask him questions,
you'll wish that you had not.

MY GAMMEE

I have an old Grandmother,
and she is big and fat.
She rolls her eyes at me and says,
"You brat, do this this and that."
You might think she is dangerous,
and wants to kill poor me.
But I know she is bluffing.
She wouldn't harm a flea.
I couldn't be afraid of her,
even if I tried.
You see, I know she loves me.
When I was sick, she cried!

My Mommoo

I have another Grannie.
Her name is Mommoo Mayne.
She's much more of a lady
than my Gammee, who spits flame.
She's smart and earns her money,
just like any man.
She loves me too, and always does
the very best she can.

Columbus

I know a boy named Columbus.
Like a little dog looking for fleas,
he scratches in papers and sticks.
He should be sailing the seas!

MARY BELLE

I know a girl named Mary Belle.
She comes in at the door,
to wash, and iron, and dust, and sweep,
and scrub so clean the floor.
When she is working in the house,
there's nothing you can lack.
God took a little extra time
to color her face black.
A black man carried the cross, for Christ.
That's more than a white man did.
The blacks will carry the weight of the world
as long as there's one, and they live.

LEMONADE

Lemonade is such a funny drink,
but a most delicious treat.
You take lemon to make it sour,
then sugar to make it sweet.
If sour and sweet is what folks want
to sip down with their food,
then why isn't it alright for me
to be both bad and good?
Stirring sweet into the sour
makes it right to drink.
Stirring good into the bad
with a switch helps too, I think.

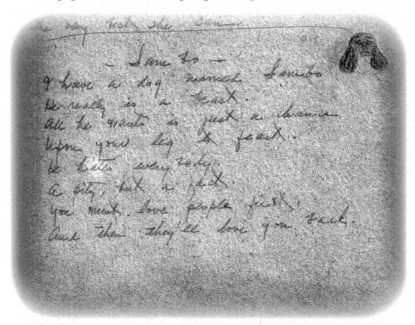

"Rory" poem and illustration by Virginia Cary Hudson Cleveland, 1953

"Sambo" poem and illustration by Virginia Cary Hudson Cleveland, 1953

RORY

I know a dog named Rory,
and he is old and good.
When I said "hello" to him,
he stopped and gently stood.
He broke his leg, poor Rory!
And that made Gammee cry.
In church she lighted a candle,
and God didn't let him die.

SAMBO

I have a dog named Sambo. He really is a beast.
All he wants is just a chance
upon your leg to feast.
He hates everybody.
A pity, but a fact.
You must love people first,
and then they'll love you back.

MY NEIGHBOR

I have a little neighbor.
I'm tired of her, you see.
So when she knocked upon my door,
just to visit with me,
I hid from her, and crept away.
I did not open my door.
Until she left, I stood quite still,
there upon my floor.
Sometime I may be knocking,
in need, upon *her* door.
Then she may stand, until I leave,
there upon *her* floor.
I had better run, to let her in,
in haste across my floor.
My need may very urgent be,
when I knock on her door.

"Dancing Girl" poem and illustration by Virginia Cary Hudson Cleveland, 1953

THE DANCING GIRL

I watched an enchanting dancer,
as around the stage she sped.
First she was upon her feet,
and then upon her head.

"Friendship" poem by Virginia Cary Hudson Cleveland, 1953

"If" poem and giraffe illustration by Virginia Cary Hudson Cleveland, 1953

FRIENDSHIP

Friendship is a priceless thing
different from everything else.
You can not buy it, and if you earn it
you must forget yourself.
You seek it where it should be,
in a long familiar face,
then you find it in another
least suspected place.
If you really want a friend,
here's all you have to do.
Just start being a friend yourself.
Try it! You'll find it's true.

IF

If I were a giraffe,
I would not have to go,
upstairs to see,
what I want to know.

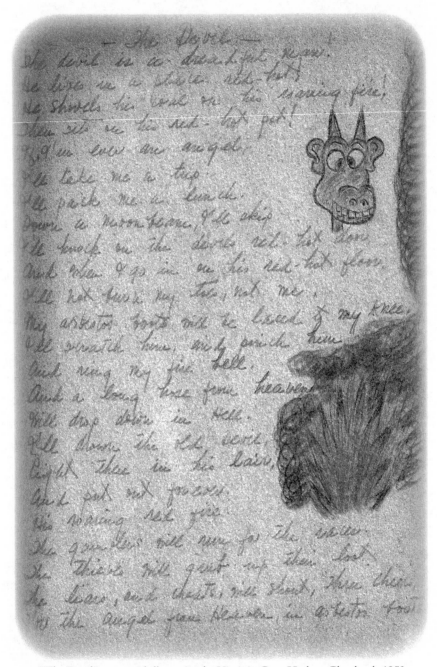

"The Devil" poem and illustration by Virginia Cary Hudson Cleveland, 1953

THE DEVIL

The devil is a dreadful man!
He lives in a place red-hot!
He shovels his coal on his roaring fire!
Then sits on his red-hot pot!
If I'm ever an angel,
I'll take me a trip.
I'll pack me a lunch.
Down a moonbeam I'll skip.
I'll knock on the devil's red-hot door,
and when I go in on his red-hot floor,
I'll not burn my toes, not me.
My asbestos boots will be laced to my knee.
I'll scratch him, and pinch him,
and ring my fire bell.
And a long hose from Heaven
will drop down in Hell.
I'll drown the old devil,
right there in his lair
and put out forever
his roaring red fire.
The gamblers will run for the races.
The thieves will grab up their loot.
The liars, and cheats, will shout, three cheers,
for the angel from Heaven, in asbestos boots!

"Market Level" illustration by Virginia Cary Hudson Cleveland, 1953

THE FINISH

I have a horse, a beautiful horse;
Market Level is his name.
He spread his nostrils, and gathered his speed,
and raced down the track to fame.
If you, in the winners' circle, would stand,
you can't just putter, and sit.
You must pound out your heart and hoofs, on the turf.
A thoroughbred does not quit.
If Fate beats you to the outside,
and you lose your place on the rail.
If, at the wire, you get nosed out,
don't feel that you have failed.
God looks down on the Race of Life.
He sees when you're left at the post.
He can tell when some one pulls you.
He knows who is trying the most.
He senses the girth of circumstance,
buckled about you, too tight.
He feels the weight upon your back,
as you strain with all your might.
He knows what odds are against you,
and when your feet slip in Life's mud.
He knows the difference in going that's tough
and a track that is fast and good.
'Tis God who will be in the judge's stand.
He sees who gives, and who hoards.
The numbers that go up in Heaven
may not be those on the boards.
When the saddle is thrown across your back,
to this promise of God hold fast.
"The last shall be first," He plainly tells you,
and also, "The first shall be last."

The Grasshopper

I saw a green grasshopper
a-fixin for to jump.
He said to me, "How do you do?"
And I said, "Oh, shut up!"
Now why should I be rude to him?
For my plight, he's not to blame.
And, when I thought it over,
I was very much ashamed.

ONE DAY

These rhymes may now
quite senseless seem,
but one day you'll know
what they mean.
If in them you find anything
to pass on to another,
the one who will be very proud
will be your old Grandmother.

"The Stag" poem and illustration by Virginia Cary Hudson Cleveland, 1953

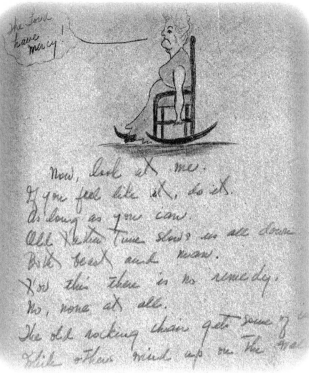

*"The Rocking Chair" poem and illustration by
Virginia Cary Hudson Cleveland, 1953*

OLD FATHER TIME

Did you ever feel like running and jumping?
So did he.
I used to feel like running and jumping.
Now, look at me.
If you feel like it, do it,
as long as you can.
Old Father Time slows us all down
both beast and man.
For this there is no remedy.
No, none at all.
The old rocking chair gets some of us,
while others wind up on the wall.

"The Madonna" poem and illustration by Virginia Cary Hudson Cleveland, 1953

THE MADONNA

A woman, on canvas, sits thru the ages
with a child pressed to her breast.
Her arms are folded about Him.
In protective quiet He rests.
She bends forward, as to shield Him.
In her eyes is piteous grace.
Her concern for His whole lifetime
is written on her face.
She represents a lasting Love,
unequaled by another.
As long as you live, never speak
unkindly to your Mother.

"Today" poem and illustration by Virginia Cary Hudson Cleveland, 1953

TODAY

Some flowers sit here on my table.
I thought I heard them sigh.
"Enjoy me today," they said,
"Tomorrow, I shall die."
All things should be enjoyed today,
that we both hear and see,
lest we become so sorry,
when they no longer be.
Enjoy all the good things now.
Don't stop with just the flowers.
One day, all the years you've lived,
will only seem like hours.

Conclusion

"Everywhere something, always to learn."
—Virginia Hudson Cleveland

I knew my grandmother barely seven years. But how I loved her! She infused my soul with her love, her strong spirit, her warmth and humor, and her expansive appreciation of the people and world around her. I try to approach new situations and places with the attitude she expressed when leaving Las Vegas in 1953: "I have never been anywhere, any time, that I have not found something to enjoy, and something in which there was sufficient good to always remember, plus, everywhere something, always to learn."

A multifaceted portrait of a fascinating and gifted woman emerges from the study of Virginia Cary Hudson's writings and from the recollections of those who knew her. Her letters brim with excitement, sorrow, and adventure. Her portraits of people, razor-sharp physical details with a piercing gaze into their souls, animate her writings as they did her conversations. Her descriptions of places and events capture significant elements that reveal the core of situations. While politeness constituted the cornerstone of good behavior for Virginia, she acted swiftly when people deserved a reprimand, and she weighed the outcome she anticipated over the risk and over unconventional behavior. Virginia, the tempered but still spirited adult, let the air out of the tires of illegal parkers who showed no respect for safety rules at St. James Court in Louisville.

The perspective I have gained on my grandmother by studying her writings for adults dwells side by side in my heart with the memory instilled in my childhood and nurtured by my mother. I recall fondly the adventures Gammee created for me. In the midst of an active household filled with family and visitors, she shaped special moments for the two of us, our own outings and activities. On trips to the live poultry market in Louisville, "the rooster store" as she called it, roosters crowed, chickens flapped and squawked, and feathers flew like snowflakes. While we crossed the bridge from Kentucky to Indiana, the state where my great-grandmother Jessie Hudson reportedly "couldn't get her breath," we each chewed a caramel marshmallow candy as fast as we could. The caramel confections, named for the Polish actress Helena Modjeska, were created in Louisville in the 1880s and still delight many children and adults today. It was hard to finish one gooey Modjeska before reaching the opposite riverbank, especially in the midst of smiles and giggles. We adopted Donald, a duck that waddled around the pantry and kitchen of the big house in St. James Court and went for walks in the yard. In quieter moments, my grandmother dressed her long gray hair with rhinestone-covered combs, she brushed my hair, and we squirted perfume on each other. We tried on hats in front of the mirror on her mahogany dressing table, carefully selecting the proper hat pins to secure them. I still have a few of those hat pins as well as a few silver-topped boxes from the dresser.

Dinners were often grand occasions with family, extra guests, and helpers laughing and singing in the kitchen. Bounded by a large pantry and a porch on one side, and a hallway and the dining room on the other, the kitchen hosted all sorts of activities unfamiliar to me. I stayed away from there when poultry was prepared the old-fashioned way, resulting in much loud squawking. Beyond the kitchen and the pantry, men would knock on the back door, asking for a hot meal, and I would come to the edge of the kitchen to peer out and see them eating on the porch or in the pantry. In the dining room, Gammee instructed me in proper table setting even before I could see the top of the table. At my place we set a wooden apple with a removable top. The apple, a bit over three inches high, still shows its red and pale yellow color. Inside the apple, she loaded nickels. If my table manners proved acceptable at dinner, I could open the apple at the end of the meal and take a nickel as my reward. If I acted up during the meal, Gammee had merely to give me a stern look and then direct her gaze with a smile to the apple. I knew what she meant; there was no need for embarrassing harsh words in front of all the table guests. Naughtiness at the table meant no nickel!

My mother, father, and I celebrated Christmas and Derby Day in Kentucky, a sort of pilgrimage from Maryland, whether by car over the mountains or by train. My mother and I traveled first by train, and my father followed by car for the days he could get free from work. What is more, my baptism took place in Kentucky, six months after my birth, and my tonsils were removed in a Louisville hospital. My mother never felt that the Washington, DC, area was "home," and that sentiment stayed with me too. She longed for her mother's presence, the source of love and faith in her life, and for the house that embraced us all. The Christmas tree in Louisville, always grand, stood in the living room to the side of the entry to one of the enclosed porches. On another side of the room, the fireplace kept us warm on cold evenings when Gammee and I warmed our "whole self," as the song says, while singing and dancing the hokeypokey. What an adventure it was for me on Christmas morning to tiptoe from the third floor all the way down the back stairs, edging by the rooms where my parents and grandparents slept and avoiding the central staircase and the landing. At last I would turn quietly and apprehensively from the hall into the living room to see what was under the tree. Auntie always followed close behind.

I treasure all these memories from the house at 1453 St. James Court. A poem that my grandmother wrote captures the tender memories of a cherished place that dwells in the heart.[167]

Home

One day I crossed, for the last time,
A threshold dear to me.
I closed a door, and in its lock
I turned my whole life's key.
Released, caressing, the knob,
Enclosing, I thought, fast
The precious memories of the years
The echoes of the Past.
Sometimes when I am tired, I see
The patterned sunlight on the floor,
I hear again the sigh of wind,
And drenching rain, against the door.
These things I thought I left behind,
Have all come here to live with me.
Instead of locking fast that door
In my own heart I turned the key.

My grandmother did not live to lock the door of 1453 St. James Court forever behind her, but she did have to close the cherished country home near Cloverport after her father's death. Her poem captures the power of preserving memories in the heart, whether of places, people, or everyday occurrences like sunlight, wind, and rain. There within us the people and places we cherish seem to flow together.

My grandmother also instilled lessons for life deeply within me, the sort of lessons found in her scrapbook for me and in her letters. Some of the most striking images my grandmother used in her writing relate to horse racing. Rooted in the everyday life she spent with my grandfather, her racing images tie together faith and hope with a view of life's hard bumps, sharp turns, and downright unfairness. The ups and downs of horse racing bring to mind the uneven course of life as well as its end at the Judgment.

In the poem "The Finish," my grandmother compares the hard moments in life to a horse slipping in the mud, getting left at the post, losing a place on the rail, and getting nosed out at the wire.

In order to win, she advises, "You must pound out your heart and hoofs, on the turf." Yet a horse or a human may try hard and still lose because of the great obstacles at the track and in life. "God looks down on the Race of Life," though, and knows the difficulties. God will be a kind and fair judge at life's end. On the course of salvation, unlike the racetrack, "'The last shall be first,' He plainly tells you, / and also, 'The first shall be last.'"

Finally, my grandmother brings together the jockey's conduct on the track and people's treatment of each other. One of her letters describes a race during which a rival jockey pushed the rider of my grandfather's horse onto the track. My grandfather lodged a protest in order to request an inquiry, a review of the race. However, the judge said he never saw it happen and refused to call the inquiry.[168] The just judge, however, will not reward dishonest behavior, she asserts: "When the course of our lives is run and we cross the finish line, if we have, in our running, bumped and hindered those alongside of us and made their going harder, although we may win, the victory will be ashes on our tongues" (*Close Your Eyes*, 68).

Virginia found ingenious solutions to make the going easier for people she knew and people she encountered by chance. Although my grandmother confronted robbers more than once, most of the strangers she wrote about were not threatening. Moreover, she had a keen sense of when her intervention would help someone. The letters published in *Flapdoodle* recount some instances of her assistance to strangers. Over and over she responded to the question, "Whom have you as a stranger taken in?" (*Flapdoodle*, 28–29).

My grandmother brought together the everyday and the spiritual in real and fanciful ways. Her Good Friday preaching to her church aimed right for the back of the parishioners' closets, where they stuffed old clothing that could clothe someone in need. She reminded them that "bums and tramps," if that was what they called them, were "just as much children of God" as they were. Strangers, she explained, included not only the hungry and thirsty but people of different opinions, faith, education, culture, and race. Virginia reminded her listeners that there were "six other days" than Sunday "to be lived before we return" to church. She lamented that there were very few people in the world who cared about doing anything for anybody. She believed in heavenly aid in daily life, and she stayed alert for the chance to provide assistance herself.

My grandmother believed in angels, believing that they serve as messengers to those who "have eyes that see and ... have ears that hear." Angels, she attested, had nudged her arm, pointed her in the right direction, placed her head on their shoulders, cheered her up, and wiped the tears from her eyes. She imagined angels having fun, and she mused about what she would do if she became one: she would have wings and a harp, and she would fly over the oceans and "wave at the sea gulls and the eagles." The angels she depicted also flew low to dip their toes in the cool waters of a lake, and they flew over houses of friends to check on them. She linked the heavenly to the earthly in their flight, destinations, and delights.

From angels down to flowers and squirrels, my grandmother's writings brought to life God's creation. From my grandmother's point of view, the stars represented God's blessings and reminded us that we owe gratitude to God for everything. She conveyed the voices and feelings of creatures—an owl, a flower, a squirrel, a duck. She never lost her childlike wonderment at creation, and she imparted it to me in her letters and drawings and during the time we spent together. She gave a voice to objects that she and I both knew, such as the pink swing on the porch, my stick horse, and my doll buggy. She had many paintings and reproductions of the Virgin Mary and of Mary and Jesus hanging on the walls, and she gave them opinions too. She remarked to my mother before meetings at her home, "The mothers of God I have on the walls will all need the glass washed over their faces, so that Mary can get a good look at the hypocrites. The new [view on] church unity for the Episcopalians is for the other churches to let *them* be boss. I hope that Jesus has a sense of humor!"[169] Imaginative, fun-loving, and acutely perceptive, Virginia brought joy, humor, care, and compassion to the people she knew and met by chance. Her writings gave emotions to the things around her and made them conversation partners in a universe filled with beauty and mystery as well as hope in the face of illness and death.

The openness to beauty and adventure that my grandmother expressed upon leaving Las Vegas animated her life and her writings. "Enjoy me today," a flower told her, for "tomorrow, I shall die." The sense of tragedy in life and the imminence of death permeated her thought—the loss of her infant son, the sudden heart attack that took her father's life, the deaths of so many young Kentucky men in the wars, the grief over Sallie and William, the fire at 1453 St. James Court, the stable fires that consumed beautiful animals and human aspirations, the constant pain of kidney stones grinding inside her, and the continuing worries about her health. As early as 1946, she described herself to my mother as an old woman.[170] The belief in the miraculous and the hope within this life and for eternal life sustained her and balanced the weight of sadness and chronic pain.

One summer as she journeyed to Johns Hopkins, my grandmother faced nearly certain and dangerous surgery on both kidneys.[171] It so happened that the day my grandmother arrived, two leading urologists were visiting the hospital—one from London and the other from the Mayo Clinic in Minnesota. When the physicians learned of her case, both offered to join the Hopkins team and to donate their services to help her. As the anesthesia begin to dull her senses, she recited the Twenty-third Psalm. She awoke and thanked the doctors, whereupon the English physician replied, "It is you who have helped yourself and us, because this operation we have performed without surgery is due only to the grace of God." I do not know exactly what happened. A photocopied postcard (undated) to my mother reads that my grandmother was not going to require surgery but that she had gone to the operating room three times for kidney drainage. In letters sent from Baltimore in the summer of 1952, my grandmother alerted my auntie Ann that the medical team would be trying to extract stones from her, naming a Dr. Howard as the physician. Whatever the procedure and whatever year it occurred, it allowed her to avoid a risky operation and relieved some pain.

My grandmother explained in a talk to her Sunday school class that she did not "think that God sent one man across the ocean and another across the country" for her sake; nor did she believe that she had any special standing in God's eyes. However, she did believe that "God sent her to the table on the one day those men were scheduled to be at the hospital" and that "we do not earn or deserve the love of God; we already have it." She concluded the class with a humorous remark: "An experience such as I have just described—and there have been others—may explain why I have so much to say in the measly thirty minutes I am allotted each Lord's Day" (*Close Your Eyes*, 60–62).

I give thanks that my grandmother lived nearly sixty years and had "so much to say" in the writings that my mother carefully preserved and published. Nina Sankovitch in *Signed, Sealed, and Delivered*, observes about letters that

> when I write a letter, I begin the equation, I open the circle, I take a step toward connection. Writing a letter is a kind of redemption mixed in with creation, mixed in with faith, absolute faith that I will travel across miles and bring me close to the one I write to.[172]

Circle, connection, creation, faith, closeness: my grandmother's letters, drawings, and other writings connect me to her as they did to my mother, and from me they extend to my daughter. They bind us in a circle, a close connection that celebrates divine and human creation and reaffirms what we have transmitted from one generation to the next. Through her writings, my grandmother still teaches me about the joy and sadness in human life and expresses for me the unity and wonder of God's universe, from the ants in the yard to the angels in heaven. My mother's publication of my grandmother's writings, against all odds, teaches the strength of love and prayer and the power of resilience. My book serves in part as a letter to my grandmother and to my mother, as it gives thanks for their love, faith, and teaching. Their letters traveled across miles. My book touches them across time. Glory three times also and amen twice!

List of Illustrations

15. William sitting on the running board of the "Ida Red," with a dog on either side, undated
16. Jessie Gregory Hudson and R. N. Hudson, 1910
17. R. N. Hudson with two dogs, undated
18. Virginia Cleveland and Ann Cleveland, holding a small dog, probably summer 1923
19. Virginia Cleveland and Ann Cleveland riding a pony while their grandfather R. N. Hudson holds the reins, August 1923
20. 1929 L. H. & St. L. pass for family members of R. N. Hudson
21. R. N. Hudson (*second from right*) and others with the number 359 car of the L & N railroad
22. Virginia Cary Hudson Cleveland and Kirtley S. Cleveland in Versailles, Kentucky, between 1913 and 1915
23. Virginia Cary Hudson Cleveland in Versailles, Kentucky, between 1913 and 1915
24. Virginia Cary Hudson Cleveland, age twenty-two, 1917
25. Kirtley S. Cleveland on horseback with two thoroughbreds and two jockeys, date unknown, ca. 1940–1950
26. Kirtley S. Cleveland at the racetrack, 1950s
27. Kirtley S. Cleveland (*second from left*) and three other men at the Tropical Garden in Havana, Cuba, 1928
28. Street view in Cuba, 1928
29. Virginia Cleveland (*center*) and Ann Cleveland (*second from right*) posing with three other girls (unidentified) in Cuba, 1928
30. Ann Cleveland (*far left*) and Virginia Cleveland (*second from right*) sitting with three other girls (unidentified) in Cuba, 1928
31. Virginia Cleveland (*left*) and Ann Cleveland (*right*) on a rooftop terrace in Cuba, 1928
32. Ann Cleveland (*left*) and Virginia Cleveland (*right*) on the beach in Marianao, Cuba, 1928
33. Virginia Cleveland (*left*), Juanita (*center*), and Ann Cleveland (*right*) at the front gate of the house in Cuba, 1928
34. Virginia Cleveland (*left*), Juanita (*center*), and Ann Cleveland (*right*) beneath palm trees in Cuba, 1928

3. *Left to right:* Lewis Mayne, Betty Bartelme, James Gregg, Beverly Mayne, Virginia Mayne, Doris Thompson, and Martha Johnson, 1962
4. Virginia Cleveland Mayne riding a camel in Egypt while holding *O Ye Jigs & Juleps!*, March 1963
5. A typical rapid signature from Virginia on a postcard: "Love, Mother"
6. A drawing of an unhappy face that closes a letter
7. A drawing of Virginia with new earrings that closes a letter

Chapter 5

1. Self-portrait by Virginia Cary Hudson Cleveland, 1952
2. Drawing of a squirrel by Virginia Cary Hudson Cleveland, 1952
3. Drawing of the buggy carriage by Virginia Cary Hudson Cleveland, 1952
4. Drawing of a sucker candy by Virginia Cary Hudson Cleveland, 1952
5. Drawing of Pal, the Stick-Horse, by Virginia Cary Hudson Cleveland, 1952
6. Virginia's drawing of herself as an angel, 1952
7. Drawing of the Ascension by Virginia Cary Hudson Cleveland, 1952
8. Cover of Scrapbook, "Sitting and Thinking," 1953
9. "A Red Bird" illustration by Virginia Cary Hudson Cleveland, 1953
10. "A Little Flower" illustration by Virginia Cary Hudson Cleveland, 1953
11. "A Blue Bird" illustration by Virginia Cary Hudson Cleveland, 1953
12. "In Kentucky" illustration by Virginia Cary Hudson Cleveland, 1953
13. "A Little Owl" illustration by Virginia Cary Hudson Cleveland, 1953
14. "A Yard" illustration by Virginia Cary Hudson Cleveland, 1953

15. "Rory" poem and illustration by Virginia Cary Hudson Cleveland, 1953
16. "Sambo" poem and illustration by Virginia Cary Hudson Cleveland, 1953
17. "Dancing Girl" illustration by Virginia Cary Hudson Cleveland, 1953
18. "Friendship" poem by Virginia Cary Hudson Cleveland, 1953
19. "If" poem and giraffe illustration by Virginia Cary Hudson Cleveland, 1953
20. "The Devil" poem and illustration by Virginia Cary Hudson Cleveland, 1953
21. "Market Level" illustration by Virginia Cary Hudson Cleveland, 1953
22. "The Stag" poem and illustration by Virginia Cary Hudson Cleveland, 1953
23. "The Rocking Chair" poem and illustration by Virginia Cary Hudson Cleveland, 1953
24. "The Madonna" poem and illustration by Virginia Cary Hudson Cleveland, 1953
25. "Today" poem and illustration by Virginia Cary Hudson Cleveland, 1953

Endnotes

1 Letter is dated Thursday the sixteenth, probably October 1952, but no month or year is given. The original was given to the Kentucky Historical Society and sealed for twenty-five years after Virginia Mayne's death (1989), until 2014.

2 Virginia Cary Hudson Cleveland to her daughter Virginia, 18 September 1952, in the author's possession.

3 "Frightened Horses Run Wild as Fire Sweeps Waterford," *Pittsburgh Post-Gazette*, October 17, 1952.

4 Citizens Fidelity Insurance Company to Virginia Cleveland Mayne, 26 July 1962, in the author's possession.

5 Kentucky Historical Society Archives, not yet in catalog. Catalogs accessed November 17, 2015, http://history.ky.gov/search-our-collections/.

6 A San Diego newspaper writer claimed to remember Virginia as a newspaper writer in New York. See note 117 on Stuart Lake. The statement about Virginia earning a precarious living was written for the inside book cover of *Flapdoodle, Trust & Obey* by someone at Harper & Row without my mother's knowledge or approval.

7 Data from 1880 census for District 2. Jessie's siblings were Ernest, ten; Louisa, seven; and Sallie, three. Nellie Hambledon, mixed race, also resided with them. Eliza's birthplace was given as Indiana and her father's as New York.

8 Photos of Cloverport are available at Kentucky Historical Society, accessed November 19, 2015, http://www.kyhistory.com/cdm/search/searchterm/Cloverport%20%28Ky.%29/mode/exact/order/description.

9 "Valuable Dog Passes Away," *Breckenridge News*, June 6, 1900.

10 Janet Lowell Walker, "Jigs, Juleps—And a Little Girl," review of *O Ye Jigs & Juleps!*, by Virginia Cary Hudson, *Louisville Courier Journal*, April 29, 1962, 7–8.

11 Virginia Cary Hudson Cleveland to her daughter Virginia, quoted in Virginia Cary Hudson, *Flapdoodle, Trust & Obey* (Harper & Row, 1966), 56.

12 According to family records, Richard Nathaniel Hudson IV was the son of Nora Doyle and R. N. Hudson III. He was born in Manchester, England, in 1810; came to New York City in 1831; became a naturalized citizen; and then pursued a career as a physician surgeon in Richmond, Virginia. He married Ann(e) Cary in St. John's Church in Richmond. He and Ann are both buried at the estate known as Woodbourne in Louisa, Virginia.

13   Data from 1860, 1870, and 1880 censuses. Ann Cary was the daughter of Miles Cary (1797/8–1849), son of another Miles Cary (1763–1797), who was the son of Richard Cary (1734–1789). Richard was the son of yet another Miles Cary (1701–1766), who was the son of yet another Miles Cary (1655–1708) (Colonel Miles Cary or Miles Cary Jr.). Cynthia Swope, "The Cary Family of England and Virginia: Our American Carys and Their European Forebears," *Within the Vines*, accessed November 17, 2015, http://www.cynthiaswope.com/withinthevines/CaryFamily/TitlePage.html.

14   Signature book from Eastman College. Report card from Richmond school.

15   Cynthia Swope, "The Cary Family of England and Virginia: Our American Carys and Their European Forebears," *Within the Vines*, accessed November 17, 2015, http://www.cynthiaswope.com/withinthevines/CaryFamily/TitlePage.html. Wilson Miles Cary (1733–1817) and Sarah Blair had five children, including a son named Miles Cary, b. 1766 (*Virginia Gazette*, April 21, 1774). Anne Robinson (March 2, 1775–November 25, 1842) was the wife of Richard Cary, married 1797 in York County, Virginia, and the mother of Miles (1798–1849), who married Harriet Staples (unknown date), who bore nine children. The sixth child and first daughter was Ann Cary, who married R. N. Hudson IV.

16   Hugh Blair Grigsby, *The Virginia Convention of 1776* (Richmond, VA: J. W. Randolph, 1855), http://archive.org/stream/virginiaconvention00grigrich/virginiaconvention00grigrich_djvu.txt.

17   "The Lady of Belvoir," *Virginia Living*, accessed November 17, 2015, http://www.virginialiving.com/virginiana/history/the-lady-of-belvoir/; Maggie MacLean, "Sally Carry Fairfax," *History of American Women* (blog), January 3, 2009, http://www.womenhistoryblog.com/2009/01/sally-cary-fairfax.html; "From George Washington to Sarah Cary Fairfax, 13 February 1758," Founders Online, National Archives, accessed November 17, 2015, http://founders.archives.gov/documents/Washington/02-05-02-0065.

18   Virginia Cary Hudson Cleveland to "Dear Brat" (her daughter Virginia), n.d., in the author's possession. This undated letter was probably given to my mother, as there is no sign of mailing. It recounts what Harriet Cary had written about the family in Virginia and about the two tables that Miles Cary, the immigrant, and a later Miles presumably brought from England.

19   Obituary in Jessie Gregory Hudson's hand, with R. N. Hudson's materials from Ann Cleveland.

20   The Old Tombigbee River Bridge, built in 1927, was restored in 2013 as a pedestrian walkway. William Browning, "Crowd Celebrates Restored Old Tombigbee Bridge," *Dispatch*, October 19, 2013, http://www.cdispatch.com/news/article.asp?aid=28118&TRID=1&TID=#ixzz35OqbYkkM.

21 Clara Cox, "William MacFarland Patton, Soldier, Engineer, Teacher, Administrator," *Virginia Tech Magazine* (Winter 2009), http://www.vtmag.vt.edu/winter09/retrospect.html.

22 A camelback truss bridge over the Green River: "Berry Bridge," accessed November 17, 2015, http://bridgehunter.com/ky/green/berry/. Near Cloverport, the smaller Blackford Creek Bridge was built in Hancock County around 1920.

23 Obbie Todd, "Green River, One of the Last Wilderness Rivers in the U.S.," *Outdoor Adventure Blog*, September 19, 2011, http://adventureblog.kentuckytourism.com/2011/09/19/green-river-one-of-the-last-wilderness-rivers-in-the-u-s/.

24 The bridge, pictured fully open, rotates one way to allow trains to pass over and rotates another way to disconnect itself from the main rail line to let barges pass. See also James Baughn, "Spottsville Railroad Bridge," accessed November 17, 2015, http://bridgehunter.com/ky/henderson/spottsville-railroad/.

25 "Louisville, Henderson and St. Louis Railway Company building, Louisville, Kentucky, 1913," University of Louisville Libraries, accessed November 19, 2015, http://digital.library.louisville.edu/cdm/singleitem/collection/cs/id/1160/rec/8. Photo of L. H. & St. L. Railway Company building at Second and Main Streets, Louisville.

26 R. N. Hudson's career is documented in numerous newspaper and magazine clippings and in a 1916 reference book for the press: *Press Reference Book of Prominent Kentuckians* (Louisville KY: Standard Printing Company, 1916), 141.

27 The use of handcars declined around 1910 in favor of the motorized speeder car. Mason Clark, "Railroad Handcar," accessed November 17, 2015, http://www.railroadhandcar.com/history/. Daimler invented a motorized handcar in 1887. "1887 Daimler motorized handcar.jpg," uploaded March 29, 2008, https://commons.wikimedia.org/wiki/File:1887_Daimler_motorized_handcar.jpg.

28 *Wikipedia*, s.v. "Fairbanks-Morse," last modified October 5, 2015, http://en.wikipedia.org/wiki/Fairbanks-Morse.

29 *Wikipedia*, s.v. "James Ben Ali Haggin," last modified October 6, 2015, http://en.wikipedia.org/wiki/James_Ben_Ali_Haggin. James Ben Ali Haggin (December 9, 1822–September 13, 1914) was an attorney, rancher, investor, and a major owner/breeder of thoroughbreds.

30 *Wikipedia*, s.v. "Joseph Hodges Choate," last modified October 15, 2015, http://en.wikipedia.org/wiki/Joseph_Hodges_Choate. Joseph Hodges Choate (1832–1917) was an influential lawyer and diplomat.

31 *Wikipedia*, s.v. "Elmendorf Farm," last modified August 24, 2015, https://en.wikipedia.org/wiki/Elmendorf_Farm.

32 *Wikipedia*, s.v. "James Ben Ali Haggin," last modified October 6, 2015, http://en.wikipedia.org/wiki/James_Ben_Ali_Haggin. Margaret Hall School in Versailles was named for Margaret Pearl Voorhies, second wife of Haggin. According to her obituary in the *Courier Journal*, she married Mr. Haggin when he was seventy-four. He died in 1914 at age ninety-two; she was nearly ninety-six when she died.

33 Photocopy of article, undated: "R. N. Hudson Builds Home in Hancock."

34 Ibid.

35 "Valuable Dog Passes Away," *Breckenridge News*, June 6, 1900.

36 1936 diary; last check from Pendennis with stamped date and Jessie Gregory's handwriting on the back.

37 Rick Bell, *The Great Flood of 1937: Rising Waters, Soaring Spirits* (Louisville, KY: Butler Books, 2007).

38 Virginia Cary Hudson Cleveland to her daughter Virginia, [1946], in the author's possession.

39 Virginia Cary Hudson Cleveland to her daughter Virginia, [1947], in the author's collection.

40 Virginia Cary Hudson Cleveland to her daughter Virginia, n.d., in the author's possession. Virginia Cary Hudson Cleveland included a transcription of Carrie's telephone conversation in this letter.

41 Ebay, accessed November 19, 2015, http://www.ebay.ie/sch/sis.html?_nkw=Antique%201928%20Post%20Card%20Tropical%20Garden%20Havana%20Cuba&_itemId=271404540084.

42 Gustavo Pérez Firmat, "Havana Mañana: Cuba in the American Imagination," *Cubainfo* (lecture series, Cuban Research Institute, Florida International University, Miami, June 2008), quoted in Gustavo Pérez Firmat, *The Havana Habit* (New Haven and London: Yale University Press, 2010). See "Gustavo Pérez Firmat," accessed November 19, 2015, http://www.gustavoperezfirmat.com/gpf_books.php.

43 César J. Ayala, "Social and Economic Aspects of Sugar Production in Cuba, 1880–1930," *Latin American Research Review* 30, no. 1 (1995): 95–124. In 1913, the thirty-nine American-owned sugar mills represented 23 percent of the sugar mills in Cuba. Investments by American companies increased 536 percent between 1913 and 1928.

44 Natasha Geiling, "Before the Revolution," Smithsonian.com, July 31, 2007, http://www.smithsonianmag.com/history-archaeology/Before_the_Revolution.html#ixzz2XRlSrFAq.

45 Basile Woon, *When It's Cocktail Time in Cuba*, privately published in 1928 and available at http://www.martiniplace.com/EUVS7/CocktailCuba.html, accessed November 17, 2015, quoted in Roberto González Echeverría, *The*

Pride of Havana: A History of Cuban Baseball (New York: Oxford University Press, 1999), 163.

46 Paul Chartier, "Veradero: Al Capone Was Here—Or Was He?," Visit Cuba, February 26, 2013, http://www.visitcuba.com/2013/02/veradero-al-capone-was-here-or-was-he?. Photo credit to State Archives of Florida, Florida Memory.

47 Robert Lacey, *Little Man: Meyer Lansky and the Gangster Life* (Boston: Little, Brown, 1991). In 1937, gangster Meyer Lansky gained control of the racetrack and casino.

48 *Wikipedia*, s.v. "Oriental Park Racetrack," last modified April 26, 2014, http://en.wikipedia.org/wiki/Oriental_Park_Racetrack.

49 González Echevarría, *The Pride of Havana*, 138–39, 153. Charles Stoneham and John McGraw, owner and manager of the Giants, purchased Oriental Park in 1919. Tillinghast L'Hommedieu Houston was part owner of the New York Yankees.

50 Ibid., 164–65.

51 Ibid., 163.

52 Noble Brandon Judah, preface (written March 18, 1937) to *Diary of My Stay in Cuba* (White Bear Lake, MN, 1994), p. 4, Noble Brandon Judah Papers, Library of Congress. The chief interest in the diary of Noble Brandon Judah, ambassador to Cuba (1927–1929), lies in the entries that relate to Charles Lindbergh's visit to the island in 1929.

53 González Echevarría, *The Pride of Havana,* 165.

54 http://web-archive-ar.com/ar/o/osafweb.com.ar/2013-03-25_1718840_14/Jockey_Clubs_e_Hip_oacute_dromos/.

55 Mary Jane Gallagher, "First Call," n.d., Buckley's widow, Emma, donated land along the Kentucky River in 1967 for the Clyde E. Buckley Wildlife Sanctuary. See "Clyde E. Buckley Wildlife Sanctuary & Life Adventure Center," Central Kentucky Audubon Society, accessed November 19, 2015, http://buckleyhills.org/About_Us.html.

56 Letter from Virginia Cleveland Mayne to W. R. Buster concerning the gift of items to the Kentucky Historical Society, 28 May 1975, in the author's possession.

57 Virginia Cary Hudson Cleveland to her daughter Virginia, 18–19 September 1952, in the author's possession. Daniel Okrent, *Last Call: The Rise and Fall of Prohibition* (New York: Simon & Schuster, 2010), 146–158. Samuel Bronfman was then the owner or chief of Seagram's, which he founded.

58 "History," Bell's Health Care, accessed November 17, 2015, http://www.bells-healthcare.com/history. Bell's Healthcare was founded in England in 1847.

59 David Schmitz, "Hall of Fame Trainer Mack Miller Dies," *Blood-Horse*, December 11, 2010, http://www.bloodhorse.com/horse-racing/articles/60308/hall-of-fame-trainer-mack-miller-dies. Mack Miller worked as a foreman for Kirtley Cleveland before obtaining his trainer's license in 1949.

60 "8200 Attend Jockey Club Inaugural," *Las Vegas Sun*, September 5, 1953, http://www.lasvegassun.com/news/1953/sep/05/8200-attend-jockey-club-inaugural/?framing=history; *Wikipedia*, s.v. "Las Vegas in the 1950s," last modified September 30, 2015, http://en.wikipedia.org/wiki/Las_Vegas_in_the_1950s; and "Stables Plan Center Operations in Vegas," *Las Vegas Sun*, September 4, 1953, http://www.lasvegassun.com/news/1953/sep/04/stables-plan-center-operations-vegas/?framing=history.

61 See "History," Las Vegas Paiute Tribe, accessed November 17, 2015, http://www.lvpaiutetribe.com/history.html.

62 See Victoria Boutilier, "1956–1973," Lauritz Melchior Web, last modified July 4, 2006, http://heroictenor.com/chronology5673.html.

63 Virginia Cary Hudson Cleveland to "Dear Brat" (her daughter Virginia), [1953], in the author's possession.

64 The other Episcopal churches in Las Vegas were founded in 1960 and 1963. On Christ Church, see "History of Christ Church Episcopal—Las Vegas, NV," Christ Church Episcopal, accessed November 17, 2015, http://www.christepiscopallv.org/history/.

65 Virginia Cary Hudson Cleveland to "Dear Brat" (her daughter Virginia), [1953], in the author's possession.

66 T. S. Eliot, *Collected Poems 1909–1962* (New York: Harcourt, Brace, 1963), 156.

67 Virginia Cary Hudson Cleveland to "Dear Brat" (her daughter Virginia), [1953], in the author's possession.

68 Virginia Cary Hudson Cleveland to her daughter Virginia, [1952], in the author's possession. The letter is undated but probably from August. An August 28, 1952, letter from Virginia Cary Hudson Cleveland at the McClure Hotel, Wheeling, to her daughter Virginia includes the racing program for that day from Wheeling Downs. Kirtley possibly went from Wheeling to Toronto to test the horse and then came back.

69 George Fetherling, "Big Bill Lias," in *e-WV: West Virginia Encyclopedia*, last modified November 3, 2015, http://www.wvencyclopedia.org/articles/1373. A series of articles appeared in 2015 about organized crime in Wheeling. On William Lias, see Steve Novotney, "The Wheeling Mob: Part 9," Weelunk, September 19, 2015, http://weelunk.com/the-wheeling-mob-part-9/.

70 Virginia Cary Hudson Cleveland to "Dear Brat" (her daughter Virginia), [1952], in the author's possession.

71 Films from Keeneland are available on YouTube, as in "2013 April Two-Year-Olds In Training Sale, Hip 51," YouTube video, 3:43, posted by "Keeneland," April 8, 2013, https://www.youtube.com/watch?v=82UgYVc00mU.

72 *Kentucky Notes,* June 15, 1963.

73 Bill Mooney, "Recalling the Life of Bill Hartack," *Paulick Report,* August 5, 2011, http://www.paulickreport.com/news/people/recalling-the-life-of-jockey-bill-hartack/.

74 Virginia Cary Hudson Cleveland to her daughter Virginia, 29 May 1946, in the author's possession.

75 David Dominé, *Old Louisville: Exuberant, Elegant, and Alive,* photographs by Franklin and Esther Schmidt (Savannah, GA: Golden Coast Publishing Company, 2013), 110–11.

76 Ibid., 111.

77 Virginia Cary Hudson Cleveland to her daughter Virginia, 29 May 1946, in the author's possession.

78 Virginia Cary Hudson Cleveland to her daughter Virginia, 7 July 1946, in the author's possession.

79 Virginia Cary Hudson Cleveland to her daughter Virginia, [1946], 7 and 29 May 1946, in the author's possession.

80 Complete text in Virginia Cary Hudson, *O Ye Jigs & Juleps!* (New York: Macmillan Company, 1962), 40–44.

81 Virginia Cary Hudson Cleveland to her daughter Virginia, October 1952, in the author's possession.

82 Virginia Cary Hudson Cleveland to her daughter Virginia, n.d., in the author's possession.

83 Joan Riehm, "Fallen Lady: St. James Court Fountain Loses Its Statue," *Courier-Journal,* April 7, 1973.

84 "After the Southern Exposition closed and disassembled in 1887, the area was purchased at auction by Mr. William H. Slaughter in 1888, who then subdivided it into building lots. He formed the Victoria Land Company through which the lots were sold. Mr. Slaughter designed St. James Court to include the center greens and a fountain, which he ordered from England ... In the early 1970s the original fountain was dismantled after years of repairs had been made and had failed. The fountain was recast in bronze by Fine Arts Sculpture Centre in Clarkson, Michigan. The project took three years and the new fountain, with a newly sculpted central figure (the original was broken while dismantling it) was dedicated on September 14th, 1975. In 2010, the basin of the fountain was re-poured after the previous one had decayed beyond repair, at a cost of over $25,000." John Paul, "Old Louisville History. More Than a Monument: A Learning Experience," October 2012, http://www.jpaul.us/history/.

85   Undated newspaper articles about enforcement of parking.

86   Photocopy from service leaflet, Calvary Episcopal Church, Louisville.

87   Hudson, *Flapdoodle*, 72, 76. See also B. Kienzle and Pamela Walker, eds., *Women Preachers and Prophets through Two Millennia of Christianity* (Berkeley/ Los Angeles: University of California Press, 1998), xiii.

88   Virginia Cary Hudson Cleveland to "Dear Brat" (her daughter Virginia), [1952], in the author's possession.

89   Virginia Cary Hudson Cleveland to "Dear Brat" (her daughter Virginia), n.d., in the author's possession.

90   Virginia Cary Hudson Cleveland to "Dear Brat" (her daughter Virginia), [1946], in the author's possession.

91   Virginia Cary Hudson Cleveland to "Dear Brat" (her daughter Virginia), n.d., in the author's possession.

92   Virginia Cary Hudson Cleveland to "Dear Brat" (her daughter Virginia), n.d., in the author's possession.

93   Virginia Cary Hudson Cleveland to her daughter Virginia, n.d., in the author's possession.

94   Virginia Cary Hudson Cleveland to her daughter Virginia, n.d., in the author's possession.

95   Virginia Cary Hudson Cleveland to her daughter Virginia, n.d., in the author's possession.

96   Narrative written by Virginia Cleveland Mayne about the funeral and kept in personal folders.

97   John G. Fuller, *Saturday Review*, May 28, 1966, 7–8.

98   Psalm 34:7 (King James Version).

99   "For Elizabeth Bartelme," *New York Times*, August 12, 2008, http:// query.nytimes.com/gst/fullpage.html?res=9407EEDF153AF93 1A2575BC0A96E9C8B63.

100 Hildegard of Bingen, *The Gospel Homilies*, trans. Beverly Mayne Kienzle, with introduction by Beverly Mayne Kienzle (Collegeville, MN: Cistercian Publications/Liturgical Press, 2012).

101 Unsigned review of *O Ye Jigs & Juleps!*, by Virginia Cary Hudson, *Publishers' Weekly*, February 12, 1962, 135. The same review is marked February 26, 1962, in my mother's scrapbook. *Publishers' Weekly* included another note on April 30, 1962, reporting that three printings were run, for twenty-five thousand copies, before the publication date of April 16.

102 Unsigned review of *O Ye Jigs & Juleps!*, by Virginia Cary Hudson, *L. and N. Magazine*, October 1962, 26–27.

103 Unsigned review of *O Ye Jigs & Juleps!*, by Virginia Cary Hudson, *Life Magazine*, April 27, 1962, 17.

104 Topher Mathews, "Barnes and Noble Closing Down This Weekend," *Georgetown Metropolitan* [blog], December 29, 2011, http://georgetownmetropolitan.com/2011/12/29/barnes-and-noble-closing-down-this-weekend/.

105 *Publishers Weekly*, April 30, 1962.

106 Les Ledbetter, "Lewis Nichols, *Times* Drama Critic During World War II, Dead at 78," *New York Times*, April 30, 1982, http://www.nytimes.com/1982/04/30/obituaries/lewis-nichols-times-drama-critic-during-world-war-ii-dead-at-78.html.

107 Christ Church Book Store, 509 Scott St., Little Rock, Arkansas, 72201, (501) 537–1698.

108 Walt Disney to Virginia Cleveland Mayne, 12 July 1962, SC 627, Kentucky Historical Society Archives, http://khscatalog.kyvl.org; Sir Alec Guinness to Virginia Cleveland Mayne, 5 July 1964, SC 631, Kentucky Historical Society Archives, http://khscatalog.kyvl.org.

109 *Miami Herald*, March 1963; *Washington Daily News*, April 1963; *Courier Journal*, March 1963; and *Cleveland Press*, June 1963.

110 The *Courier Journal* announced the coming serialization on February 20, 1963.

111 "Young Ladies of 10—Here's How to Win $10," *Cleveland Press*, June 28, 1963.

112 C. C. Hartley, "The Spectator," *Record* (Reynoldsburg, OH), March 22, 1962.

113 Bishop is located in the Sierra Nevadas of Eastern California. Bishop Chamber of Commerce, *California's Eastern Sierra Fall Color Guide & Map*, accessed November 18, 2015, http://www.bishopvisitor.com/EasternSierraFallColorGuide2013.pdf.

114 The Ethel Jacobson who wrote the review is most likely the Ethel Jacobson who "wrote more than 6,000 verses, 100 articles and six books, including two about cats," notably "The Cats of Sea-Cliff Castle." "Ethel Jacobson; Author and Leader in the Arts in Orange County," *Los Angeles Times*, February 17, 1991, http://articles.latimes.com/1991-02-17/news/mn-1982_1_ethel-jacobson.

115 Wihla Hutson to Virginia Cleveland Mayne, 6 October 1962, 27 November 1962, in the author's possession.

116 *O Ye Jigs and Juleps!*, 3, 5.

117 The Shapell Manuscript Foundation holds a letter written November 19, 1935, from Wyatt Earp's widow, Josephine, to Stuart N. Lake, asking him to send her money. See *Wikipedia*, s.v. "Stuart N. Lake," last modified June 6, 2015, https://en.wikipedia.org/wiki/Stuart_N._Lake.

118 This review is not available electronically. The 1963 letter enclosed states that the review was being sent in the envelope, but the review is missing.

119 Payment records to Johnson and Thompson for excerpts of 3'33" and 3'00," dated May 15 and June 3, 1974.

120 *O Gij Polka's en Perendrups*, trans. Harriët Freezer (Amsterdam: Van Ditmar, 1963).

121 Cox to Virginia Cleveland Mayne, 23 November 1964, in the author's possession; Martha Heasley Cox, *Better Writing with Student Papers for Analysis* (San Francisco: Chandler Publishing Company, 1964), 31-32. "Etiquette at Church" opens with the student's first paragraph and then the rest is my grandmother's essay.

122 "O Ye Jigs & Juleps!," YouTube video, 5:25, posted by "tlackey56," October 18, 2009, http://www.youtube.com/watch?v=KMgK0kIF6vA.

123 Rebecca Scott to Virginia Cleveland Mayne, [1983]. I am grateful to Rebecca Scott for permission to use this letter.

124 Don Musselman, *O Ye Jigs & Juleps!: A Play with Music*, with music by Sim Broadfield (New Orleans, LA: Anchorage Press, 1992).

125 Sally J. Walker to Beverly M. Kienzle, 14 September 1989, in the author's possession.

126 "Family," *Globe Democrat* (St. Louis), October 29, 1964. No digital archive until 1976.

127 *Courier Journal*, September 26, 1965.

128 John E. Kleber, ed., *The Kentucky Encyclopedia* (Lexington, KY: University Press of Kentucky, 1992), 445.

129 David Dominé, *Old Louisville*, 111.

130 Undated clipping among Virginia Mayne's reviews and announcements about the books.

131 Elizabeth Bartelme (Macmillan editor) to Virginia Cleveland Mayne, 2 September 1964, in the author's possession.

132 Episcopal News Service, "Phyllis Edwards Ordained Priest Declared Deacon in 1964," July 10, 1980, Archives of the Episcopal Church, http://www.episcopalarchives.org/cgi-bin/ENS/ENSpress_release.pl?pr_number=80242.

133 Tim Hollis, *Loveman's: Meet Me Under the Clock* (Charleston, S.C: History Press, 2012). See Bob Carlton, "Birmingham's Old Loveman's Department Store Lives on in New Book from Historian Tim Hollis," Alabama Media Group, August 7, 2012, http://www.al.com/entertainment/index.ssf/2012/08/birminghams_old_lovemans_depar.html.

134 "Flapdoodle, Trust & Obey by Virginia Cary Hudson: Another Bestseller from a Pen Dipped in Magic," *Harper Religious Books* (New York: Harper & Row Publishers, 1965–1966), 11.

135 Anne Hitch, "'Julep' Fizz Is There, but Essence Is Varied," review of *Flapdoodle, Trust & Obey*, by Virginia Cary Hudson, *Baltimore Sun*, April 24, 1966.

136 See "Obituaries," Virginia Press Women, accessed November 15, 2015, http://www.virginiapresswomen.org/about/obituaries.

137 *News* (Wapakoneta, OH), February 18, 1966.

138 Miles A. Smith, "Book Review: Grandma's Advice is Zesty," review of *Flapdoodle, Trust & Obey*, by Virginia Cary Hudson, *Free Lance-Star* (Fredericksburg, VA), February 23, 1966; "From the Book Shelf—Wholesome Corn, and Story of a Family Named Glickman," review of *Flapdoodle, Trust & Obey*, by Virginia Cary Hudson, *Press* (Sheridan, WY), February 26, 1966; Associated Press, "Flapdoodle, Trust and Obey," review of *Flapdoodle, Trust & Obey*, by Virginia Cary Hudson, *Eagle* (Reading, PA), February 27, 1966; "Essays Tell Syrupy Tale," review of *Flapdoodle, Trust & Obey*, by Virginia Cary Hudson, *Home News* (New Brunswick, NJ), February 27, 1966; "Syrupy, but Wholesome: Grandma Has Advice for Living," review of *Flapdoodle, Trust & Obey*, by Virginia Cary Hudson, *Grand Rapids Press* (Grand Rapids, MI), March 6, 1966; "Some Advice by Grandma," review of *Flapdoodle, Trust & Obey*, by Virginia Cary Hudson, *Bridgeport Post* (Bridgeport, CT), March 6, 1966; "Grandma's Advice for Zesty Living," review of *Flapdoodle, Trust & Obey*, by Virginia Cary Hudson, *News-Journal* (Mansfield, OH), March 6, 1966; "Grandmother's Advice for Living Full Life," review of *Flapdoodle, Trust & Obey*, by Virginia Cary Hudson, *Fayetteville Observer* (Fayetteville, NC), March 6, 1966; "Books in Review," review of *Flapdoodle, Trust & Obey*, by Virginia Cary Hudson, *Enquirer and News* (Battle Creek, MI), March 6, 1966; "Book for Today," review of *Flapdoodle, Trust & Obey*, by Virginia Cary Hudson, *Public Opinion* (Chambersburg, PA), March 8, 1966; "Literary Guidepost," review of *Flapdoodle, Trust & Obey*, by Virginia Cary Hudson, *Citizen* (Key West, FL), March 10, 1966; "Jigs & Juleps Motif Revived," review of *Flapdoodle, Trust & Obey*, by Virginia Cary Hudson, *Commercial Appeal* (Memphis, TN), March 13, 1966; "Some Yesteryear Corn That's Wholesome," review of *Flapdoodle, Trust & Obey*, by Virginia Cary Hudson, *Herald-Leader* (Lexington, KY), March 20, 1966; "Some Advice for Zesty Living," review of *Flapdoodle, Trust & Obey*, by Virginia Cary Hudson, *News* (Port Arthur, TX), March 20, 1966; "Book Review: Grandma's Advice for Living," review of *Flapdoodle, Trust & Obey*, by Virginia Cary Hudson, *Centre Times* (State College and Bellefonte, PA), March 23, 1966; "Grandma's Advice for Zesty Living," review of *Flapdoodle, Trust & Obey*, by Virginia Cary Hudson, *Middletown Journal* (Middletown, OH), March 27, 1966; "Grandma's Advice for Zesty Living," review of *Flapdoodle, Trust & Obey*, by Virginia Cary Hudson, *Tulsa*

World (Tulsa, OK), April 3, 1966; "Grandma's Rule for Zesty Living," review of *Flapdoodle, Trust & Obey,* by Virginia Cary Hudson, *News* (Ada, OK), April 10, 1966; "Grandma's Advice for Zesty Living," review of *Flapdoodle, Trust & Obey,* by Virginia Cary Hudson, *Herald* (Durham, NC), April 10, 1966; "Grandma's Advice on Zesty Life," review of *Flapdoodle, Trust & Obey,* by Virginia Cary Hudson, *Chronicle* (Augusta, GA), April 17, 1966; and "New and Noteworthy," review of *Flapdoodle, Trust & Obey,* by Virginia Cary Hudson, *Columbus Sunday Dispatch* (Columbus, OH), April 24, 1966.

139 "Jigs & Juleps Motif Revived," review of *Flapdoodle, Trust & Obey,* by Virginia Cary Hudson, *Commercial Appeal* (Memphis, TN), March 13, 1966.

140 Velma S. Daniels, "Flapdoodle, Trust and Obey," review of *Flapdoodle, Trust & Obey,* by Virginia Cary Hudson, *News-Chief* (Winter Haven, FL), April 7, 1966.

141 Nancy O'Gara, "Flapdoodle Trust and Obey," review of *Flapdoodle, Trust & Obey,* by Virginia Cary Hudson, *Peninsula Herald* (Monterey, CA), February 26, 1966.

142 Harper & Row to Virginia Cleveland Mayne, 18 November 1968, in the author's possession.

143 Virginia Cary Hudson Cleveland to her daughter Virginia, n.d., in the author's possession.

144 Virginia Cary Hudson Cleveland to her daughter Virginia, n.d., in the author's possession.

145 Photocopy from service leaflet, Calvary Episcopal Church, Louisville.

146 Hudson, *Flapdoodle,* 72–76.

147 My grandmother and her source attribute the English translation of the Athanasian Creed to Lady Mary Mortley Montague, a very learned woman writer (1689–1762) who married John Stuart, Earl of Bute. Current sources attribute the translation to John, Marques of Bute, a later descendant.

148 Christopher Siriano, *The House of David, Images of America* (Charleston, SC: Arcadia Publishing, 2007). The Israelite House of David, a religious society, was cofounded by Benjamin and Mary Purnell in 1903. The members expanded from Michigan outward, and their baseball teams, wearing long hair and beards, toured rural America from the 1920s through the 1950s. See also *Wikipedia,* s.v. "House of David," last modified September 7, 2015, http://en.wikipedia.org/wiki/House_of_David_%28commune%29.

149 Reverend John L. Fort saw value in the idea and led the effort to establish Goodwill Industries of Kentucky. In 1923, the basement of Temple Methodist Church was transformed into Goodwill. See "About: Our History," Goodwill Industries of Kentucky, accessed November 18, 2015, http://www.goodwillky.org/about/our-history/.

150 Elisabeth Schüssler Fiorenza, *Bread not Stone: The Challenge of Feminist Biblical Interpretation* (Boston: Beacon Press, 1995). Elisabeth Schüssler Fiorenza differentiates between reading as a woman, which my grandmother did, and reading as a feminist with an agenda of social change—a movement that emerged and strengthened in the 1970s and 1980s.

151 Anne B. Boardman, review of *Close Your Eyes When Praying*, by Virginia Cary Hudson, *Foundations for Christian Living* (Pawling, NY), Christmas 1968.

152 Constance Page Daniel, "A Little Gem of a Book," review of *Close Your Eyes When Praying*, by Virginia Cary Hudson, *Newport News* (Newport, VA), January 12, 1969.

153 H. F. Davidson, review of *Close Your Eyes When Praying*, by Virginia Cary Hudson, *Presbyterian Record* (Toronto, Canada), January 1969.

154 *Eternity Book Service*, review of *Close Your Eyes When Praying*, by Virginia Cary Hudson, January 1969.

155 Virginia Cary Hudson Cleveland to her daughter Virginia, n.d., in the author's possession.

156 Among many slave narratives, see "Henry Bibb: Roots and Powders During Slavery Times," accessed November 18, 2015, http://www.southern-spirits.com/bibb-roots-powders-slaves.html; "Dinkie, a Conjure Doctor in Missouri, circa 1840," accessed November 18, 2015, http://www.southern-spirits.com/brown-dinkie.html; and "Slave Narrative: Tales of Conjure," accessed November 18, 2015, http://www.southern-spirits.com/avery-conjure.html.

157 Madelon Golden Schilpp was the wife of Paul Schilpp and author (with Sharon Murphy) of *Great Women of the Press*, available from Southern Illinois University Press. Madelon Schilpp has been a member of the journalism faculty at Southern Illinois University at Carbondale, a reporter for the *Chicago Sun-Times*, and a contributor to the *Chicago Tribune* and the *St. Louis Post-Dispatch*. For discussion of the papers of Paul Schlipp, a controversial philosophy professor and Methodist minister, see "Guide to the Paul A. Schilpp (1897–1993) Papers," Northwestern University Library, accessed November 18, 2015, http://findingaids.library.northwestern.edu/catalog/inu-ead-nua-archon-424.

158 A good concise Internet source is Lisa Vox, "Civil Rights Movement Timeline From 1965 to 1969," About.com, accessed November 18, 2015, http://afroamhistory.about.com/od/timelines/a/timelinelate60s.htm.

159 Virginia Cary Hudson Cleveland to her daughter Virginia, n.d., in the author's possession. Virginia Cary Hudson Cleveland included a transcription of Carrie's telephone conversation in this letter.

160 Virginia Cary Hudson Cleveland to her daughter Virginia, n.d., in the author's possession.

161 Hudson, *Flapdoodle*, 77.

162 A letter from Virginia Cleveland Mayne to the Kentucky Historical Society gives his name as William Jackson. William Jackson (November 16, 1886– October 2, 1947), private first class of the US Army, was buried in section b, site 736, in Zachary Taylor National Cemetery. A second man named William Jackson served in World War II; a third in World War II, Korea, and Vietnam; and a fourth in Korea. "Nationwide Gravesite Locator," US Department of Veterans Affairs, accessed November 18, 2015, http:// gravelocator.cem.va.gov/index.html.

163 Hudson, *Jigs*, 13–16. The buck-and-wing is a fast and flashy dance usually done in wooden-soled shoes and combining Irish clogging styles, high kicks, and complex African rhythms and steps such as the shuffle and slide; see Rusty Frank, "Tap Dance," in *Encyclopaedia Britannica*, accessed November 18, 2015, http://www.britannica.com/art/tap-dance#ref205307. On ragtime, see Frederick Hodges, "Kitten on the Keys," accessed November 18, 2015, http://www.frederickhodges.com/kittenonthekeyslinernotes.html.

164 R. Gerald Alvey, *Kentucky Bluegrass Country* (Jackson: University Press of Mississippi, 1992), 261. See also *Wikipedia*, s.v. "Beaten Biscuit," last modified November 8, 2015, http://en.wikipedia.org/wiki/Beaten_biscuit.

165 Gail Collins, *When Everything Changed: The Amazing Journey of American Women from 1960 to the Present* (New York: Little, Brown, 2009), 3, 242, 392.

166 Louie Robinson, "The Eternal Mills Brothers," *Ebony* 25, no. 11 (September 1970), 60–69; "Joe Delaney Remembers 1953: Mills Brothers at the Thunderbird," *Las Vegas Sun*, July 28, 2000, http://lasvegassun.com/ news/2000/jul/28/joe-delaney-remembers-1953-mills-brothers-at-the-t/.

167 Original in the papers of Virginia Cary Hudson Cleveland, owned by Beverly Cary Mayne Kienzle and inherited from Virginia Cleveland Mayne.

168 Virginia Cary Hudson Cleveland to "Dear Brat" (her daughter Virginia), n.d., in the author's possession.

169 Virginia Cary Hudson Cleveland to "Dear Brat" (her daughter Virginia), [1952], in the author's possession.

170 Virginia Cary Hudson Cleveland to "Dear Brat" (her daughter Virginia), [1946], in the author's possession.

171 The surname of Virginia's physician was Howard. She must have benefited over the years from the procedures developed at Hopkins by Howard A. Kelly (1858–1943), one of the original four members of the Johns Hopkins University medical faculty. Dr. Kelly, considered the founder of gynecology as a field and the inventor of the urinary cystoscope, coauthored a 1914 book in urology that gave special attention to women (Howard A. Kelly and Curtis F. Burnam, *Diseases of the Kidneys, Ureters and Bladder* [New York & London: D. Appleton & Co., 1914]). For more on Dr. Kelly's biography, see also "The

Four Founding Physicians," Johns Hopkins Medicine, accessed November 18, 2015, http://www.hopkinsmedicine.org/about/history/history5.html.

172 Nina Sankovitch, *Signed, Sealed, Delivered: Celebrating the Joys of Letter Writing* (New York; Simon & Schuster, 2014), 195.

Index

Bold denotes photo.

Fenwick, Abigail, 110
fires
    at 1453 St. James Court
        (Louisville KY, 1952),
        xiii, xvi–xvii, xviii, xix,
        32, 53, 67, 75, 76, 92, 146,
        175, 227
    in stables, 47, 48, 227
    at Waterford Park (Wheeling,
        1952), xvii–xviii, 169
Flapdoodle, Trust & Obey (V. C. H.
    Cleveland), xiii, xvi, xxiii, 1,
    70, 100, 103, 106, 107, 108,
    109–113, 114, 120, 121, 129,
    130–142, 225
flood, Ohio River (1937), 20
Foland, H. L., 90
Francis Scott Key Bookshop, 72,
    74, 83, 84, 85, 86, 88, 91, 94,
    95, 106
Frankfurter, Felix, 172
Friedan, Betty, 99
Fries, Hanny, 97
Fuller, John G., 69–70

G

Gates, Harold J., 16
General Convention of the Episcopal
    Church (1964), 99
Ginsburg, Ruth Bader, 172
Globe Democrat, 99, 100
Good Housekeeping, 69, 71
Goodwill Chapel, 57, 63, 118, 119,
    120, 121, 157, 169
Gordon, Fortuna, 50
Gordon, J. Fritz, 27
Gordon, Mrs. R. L., 80, 81
Greentree Stable, 160
Gregg, James R. (Jim), 73, **85**, 91, 92
Gregory, Eliza (grandmother), 2, 4

Gregory, Jessie Lee (mother), xiii,
    2, 3. *See also* Jessie Gregory
    Hudson
Gregory, John D. (grandfather), 2
Grosset and Dunlap, 69, 70
Guinness, Sir Alec, 92
The Guns of August (Tuchman), 93

H

Haggin, James Ben Ali, 15, 16
Haggin, Mrs., 16
Hampton, George, 55
Harcourt Brace & Co., 69
Harper & Row, xiii, 1, 69, 70, 73, 106,
    107, 108, 109, 111, 114
Harper Religious Books, 107
Harper's Magazine, 69, 70
Harry (family friend), 40
Hartack, Bill, 45, **46**
Hartley, C. C., 93
Havana-American Jockey Club,
    27, 28
Hemstead, Charles, 35, 49
Hildegard of Bingen, 75
Hill Gail (horse), 161
Hipódromo de las Américas, **33**
Hitch, Anne, 109
Holt, Joseph, 100
Horrible Herbert, 37, 38
horse racing. *See also specific racetracks*
    attempted launch of in Las
        Vegas, 36
    author's education at racetrack,
        43–48
    in Canada, 35–36
    in Cuba, 27–28, 31
    dark side of, 47
    history of, 148, 160
    impact of on V. C. H.
        Cleveland, 60

Made in the USA
Lexington, KY
26 September 2016